OLD TESTAMENT GUIDES

General Editor

R.N. Whybray

DANIEL

Other titles in this series include:

THE SECOND ISAIAH
R.N. Whybray

1 & 2 SAMUEL
R.P. Gordon

JUDGES
A.D.H. Mayes

JOB
J.H. Eaton

DANIEL

P.R. Davies

Published by JSOT Press
for the Society for Old Testament Study

1985

to Marley Close

Published by
JSOT Press
Department of Biblical Studies
The University of Sheffield
Sheffield S10 2TN
England

Printed in Great Britain
by Dotesios (Printers) Ltd.,
Bradford-on-Avon, Wiltshire.

British Library Cataloguing in Publication Data

[Bible. O.T. Daniel.*English* 1985]. Daniel.—
 (Old Testament guides, ISSN 0264-6498; 4)
 1. Bible. O.T. Daniel—Criticism, interpretation, etc.
  I. Title   II. Davies, P.R.   III. Series
  224'.506   BS1555.2

  ISBN 1-850750-02-5

CONTENTS

PREFACE

Daniel is not among the most frequently studied of Old Testament books, although it is certainly among the best known, and, among both scholars and laypeople, has long been one of the most controversial, whether as regards its 'predictions', its authorship and date, or its membership of that curious literary society of 'apocalypses'. Partly because of such controversy, its intrinsic theological and literary merits have tended to be undervalued. In this book, while attempting to do justice to all the traditional questions, I have also wished to develop those points of view which are in my opinion characteristic of biblical scholarship as currently practised, especially a sensitivity to literary values. If my comments at times seem to depart from the agenda prescribed by previous work on Daniel, I can only say that I hope I am in some cases anticipating the directions in which study of Daniel may move in the near future, especially in Chapters 6 and 7.

As is now common in Roman Catholic as well as Protestant commentaries on Daniel, only the twelve chapters found in the Hebrew Bible will be treated. I have used throughout the text of the Revised Standard Version, including its verse numbering, which varies slightly from the Hebrew at times. I have also used 'Daniel' sometimes to mean the hero and putative author, and sometimes to mean the book. I have tried to ensure that in no case is the meaning ambiguous.

University of Sheffield   Philip R. Davies
April 1984

Notes on the Bibliographies

The following abbreviations are used:

ANET	J. Pritchard, *Ancient Near Eastern Texts Relating to the Old Testament*, Princeton: Princeton University Press, 3rd edn, 1969
BASOR	*Bulletin of the American Schools of Oriental Research*
IDBS	K. Crim (ed.), *The Interpreter's Dictionary of the Bible, Supplementary Volume*, Nashville: Abingdon, 1976
IEJ	*Israel Exploration Journal*
JBL	*Journal of Biblical Literature*
JCS	*Journal of Cuneiform Studies*
JSJ	*Journal for the Study of Judaism*
JSOT	*Journal for the Study of the Old Testament*
JTC	*Journal for Theology and Church*
JTS	*Journal of Theological Studies*
OTL	Old Testament Library
OTS	*Oudtestamentische Studiën*
ST	*Studia Theologica*
VT	*Vetus Testamentum*

Full details of the works cited are given on their first appearance in the Bibliographies. In subsequent references they are cited by the surname of the author only, or, if more than one work by the same author are cited, by surname and brief title, e.g. 'Montgomery', 'Russell, *Method and Message*'.

An asterisk (*) indicates works most suitable for beginners.

General Reading

The most comprehensive commentary available in English is still that of *J.A. Montgomery, *Daniel* (International Critical Commentary), Edinburgh: T. & T. Clark / New York: C. Scribner's Sons, 1927. The following more recent commentaries in English may be especially recommended:

*E.W. Heaton, *The Book of Daniel* (Torch Bible Commentaries), London: SCM Press, 1956 (an impressively broad description of the theological and literary background)

*L.F. Hartman and A.A. Di Lella, *The Book of Daniel* (Anchor Bible), New York: Doubleday, 1977

*N. Porteous, *Daniel* (OTL), 2nd revised edition, London: SCM Press, 1979 / Philadelphia: Westminster Press (well-balanced assessment of opinions, with a useful Supplement reviewing publications since the original edition of 1962)

A. Lacocque, *The Book of Daniel*, London: SPCK, 1979 [French original, 1976] (erratic, but often brilliant, especially on the literary qualities of Daniel)

J. Baldwin, *Daniel* (Tyndale OT Commentaries), Leicester: Inter-Varsity Press, 1979 (of those commentaries which defend the 'conservative' interpretation, this is by far the best)

Important commentaries in other languages include:

O. Plöger *Das Buch Daniel* (Kommentar zum alten Testament), Gütersloh: G. Mohn, 1965

M. Delcor, *Le livre de Daniel* (Sources bibliques), Paris: Gabalda, 1971

J.J. Collins, *The Apocalyptic Vision of the Book of Daniel*, Missoula: Scholars Press, 1977, is especially recommended for general reading. It discusses most of the major issues and includes an excellent bibliography.

1

PREVIEW

DANIEL IS A VERY curious book in many respects. From almost every standpoint it presents a dual character: it contains two kinds of material, apparently intended originally for two different audiences; its contents relate to two different times and places; it has two canonical forms; and it is written in two languages.

Two kinds of material

The first half of the book (chs. 1–6) comprises a series of six stories (or five with an introduction), some of which are among the best-known in the world—the fiery furnace, the lions' den, Belshazzar's feast—while its second half presents a series of four visions which reveal the course of history leading from the Babylonian exile at the beginning of the sixth century BC to what is anticipated as the dawn of the final kingdom on earth (chs. 7, 8, 9, and 10–12). Chapters 7 and 8 survey most of this long period, dividing it into world-kingdoms; ch. 9 divides it differently, into seventy cycles of seven years each, thus interpreting a prophecy from Jeremiah about the period of Jerusalem's desolation. Chapters 10–12 comprise a single vision which deals with the fourth world-kingdom, that of the Greeks, and contains cryptic allusions to wars, campaigns and diplomatic manoeuvres, culminating in a brief but dramatic depiction of the end of the last wicked human king, a resurrection, judgment, and the exaltation of the righteous. All of these four visions indulge in successively more precise calculations of the time of the End. Because of their allusions to historical events, their symbolism and their unique character among the literature of the Old Testament, these later chapters have attracted more attention from biblical scholars than the stories, and commentaries on Daniel generally devote much space to identifying the characters and events cryptically alluded to, assessing the signification of the 'Son of Man' and the 'Saints', and pondering the origin and theological character of 'apocalyptic', of which Daniel 7–12 is often held to be the earliest example.

It has always been the case that, on the whole, the stories of the first half of Daniel have more appeal to laypeople, while the visions of the second half are more intriguing to scholars. This is no idle observation; for the stories and the visions were almost certainly *composed* for popular and scholarly audiences respectively. Moreover, the two halves each convey a different message on the same theme: the relationship between the kingdom of God and the kingdoms of men. The juxtaposition of different literary forms, intended audiences and messages creates a strong tension in the book as a whole. Is this tension deliberate? The answer is probably yes, and the challenge to critical scholarship is not only to distinguish carefully between the two contrasting parts of the book, but also to explore the positive aspect of this contrast: in other words, to do justice to the book of Daniel as a literary unit.

Two times, two places

The two halves of Daniel, in communicating different ideas in different forms, relate to different periods of time. The stories narrate the experiences of Jewish heroes living in Babylon, where many Jews had been deported by Nebuchadnezzar (to use the incorrect but traditional spelling employed in Daniel), and apparently extend no further in time than the reign of Cyrus, under whom these Jews were permitted to return to their own land in 538 BC. On the other hand, as already mentioned, the visions, although revealed to Daniel during the same timespan, penetrate beyond the historical horizons of the Babylonian exile and focus, each successive vision with increasing clarity, on the time centuries later when history will culminate in the final kingdom of God. The events preceding this moment are alluded to with sufficient clarity to show that the author had a specific date in view; and the knowledge we have of Jewish history enables us to place that date in the second century BC, at or about 166. The setting, too, has changed from Babylon to Palestine, where the expected culmination of history will come about. It is obvious that the visions are directed not to Daniel's contemporaries, but to those living at this future moment, and to Jews who are not in exile but in their own land. The instruction to Daniel to 'shut up the words, and seal the book, until the time of the end' (12.4) confirms that the audience of the whole of the book of Daniel as we have it must be sought, not in sixth-century Babylon, but second-century Palestine.

But the different settings of the two halves of Daniel have a typological as well as a chronological relationship. Nebuchadnezzar and the exiled Jews are both the *predecessors* and the *prototypes* of the persecuting monarch Antiochus IV and the persecuted Jews of Palestine centuries later. Hence what Daniel is shown of the future reflects, and is reflected in, the crisis of his own place and time. The ambivalent chronological/typological relationship between the two epochs is concretely expressed in the equation of the seventy years of exile calculated by Jeremiah with the 490 years of 'desolation of Jerusalem' which span the epoch of the world-kingdoms until their final disappearance. In other words, there are two 'exiles', and the physical exile in Babylon both foreshadows and initiates a more protracted period of exile, and of persecution, whose termination will coincide only with the fulfilment of world-history.

Now there is a danger in focusing one's attention on one or other of these periods to the detriment of the other, as the history of scholarship on Daniel demonstrates. By adopting a thoroughly *literal-historical* approach, and giving priority to the sixth-century Babylonian context of the stories, Daniel is seen as a real historical personage who actually wrote the visions, which in this case are understood as genuine prediction, revealing Daniel as one of the most important of the prophetic books. This view is extremely ancient: it is reflected in the the Greek Bible, where the book is placed at the head of the 'minor' prophets (after Ezekiel and before Hosea); Daniel is also spoken of as a prophet in the Dead Sea Scrolls and by Josephus. The same view was adopted, of course, by the Church Fathers and in subsequent Jewish and Christian interpretation. Traditional Christian teaching has found the fulfilment of Daniel's predictions in the coming of Christ or the Church, the final 'kingdom of God', but there has nearly always been a minority of Christians ready to see in the later chapters of the book allusions to contemporary events (a notorious modern example of this is Hal Lindsay's *The Late Great Planet Earth*).

On the other hand, an *historical-critical* approach gives priority to

the period to which the visions refer, and the audience of that period
which they, and the book as a unit, address. The theological rather
than historical value of the stories is emphasized, and the 'predictions'
are regarded as written after the events which they describe. This
view is by no means a modern one, but was argued by the philosopher
Porphyry in the 3rd century AD (see below). Some support for this
view is given by the place of Daniel in the Hebrew canon, where it is
found not among the prophetic books at all, but in the third division
known as 'Writings'. It is generally thought that the structure of the
Hebrew canon reflects the history of its formation, and the omission
of Daniel from the division of 'Prophets' tells against its antiquity.
There are, however, other reasons why nearly all modern scholars
agree with Porphyry, which we shall consider in Chapter 1. But in
their understandable desire to refute as thoroughly as possible the
traditional dating of the book and avoid the dangers of compromising
with the literal-historical interpretation, many critics have insisted
that the entire book is a *product* of the 2nd century BC. Yet although
both stories and visions in their literary combination can plausibly be
understood against the background of Antiochus' persecution, the
ideology of the stories alone reflects a political and social context
quite different from that of Palestine under Antiochus Epiphanes.
Hence it is likely that they originate in a world closer in time and
place to their hero Daniel than to the audience of the visions.

    The historical background of Daniel will be discussed more fully in
Chapter 2.

Two forms of the book

Not only the canonical position, but even the contents of Daniel
differ in the Hebrew and Greek versions: while English Bibles follow
the canonical order of the Greek, they preserve the Hebrew form of
the book, which contains twelve chapters. The Greek text (of which
two versions are preserved!) has three additions: the 'Song of the
Three Children', 'Susannah' and 'Bel and the Dragon'. The first of
these belongs in ch. 3 between vv. 23 and 24, and the others form (in
one Greek version) chs. 13 and 14. These 'additions' are nowadays
commonly separated from Daniel and included in the Apocrypha.
They are interesting in that they illustrate the existence of Daniel-
stories outside the canonical collection; their literary and theological
quality, however, compares rather unfavourably. They fall outside
the scope of this book.

Two languages

The Hebrew version of Daniel, with which we are concerned, uses two languages. This is perhaps the most perplexing of all the peculiarities of the book, and has taxed many a scholar's ingenuity. Daniel opens in Hebrew, switches to Aramaic in the middle of 2.4 and reverts to Hebrew at the beginning of ch. 8. Now, while the language of the Old Testament is Hebrew, which was the language of the people of Israel until their exile into Babylonia, Aramaic thereafter became their spoken language; it was a *lingua franca* in the Persian empire and remained so in the Hellenistic period. Yet throughout this period—the timespan covered by the book of Daniel—many Jewish religious writings in Palestine continued to be written in Hebrew, while during the Maccabean revolt—when Daniel is believed to have been written—there seems to have been a conscious revival of spoken Hebrew (see 2 Macc. 7.21).

The employment of two languages in Daniel has given rise to two problems in particular: first, the quality of the Aramaic and of the Hebrew, which bear upon the date and place of composition of the respective material; and second, the peculiar arrangement of the Hebrew and Aramaic parts within the book, which bear upon the literary structure and literary history of the book as a whole. Needless to say, both these problems have played their part in the debate about the so-called 'authenticity' of the book. We shall look more closely at the problem of the languages in Chapter 3.

II

While no external reference to the book of Daniel or its contents is known to us before the second century BC, it has exerted a tremendous influence upon Jewish literature and theology from that time onwards. For a book whose historical relevance would seem to have been lost after the end of Antiochus' persecution, this impact is rather surprising. 1 Maccabees (late second century BC), in describing Antiochus' altar as the 'abomination of desolation', is presumably quoting Daniel 9.27 // 11.31; if so, then the original historical application of the phrase is still in operation: the author knows to what Daniel was referring. But allusions to Daniel in Jewish works written in and outside Palestine—the Sibylline Oracles and Wisdom from the (Hellenized) Jews of Egypt, the Psalms of Solomon and the Qumran literature from Palestine—show that its descriptions of the closing moments of history were adopted as a model for eschatological description and reapplied to yet future events; its references were reinterpreted so that it could still address the future. What Daniel 9 did to Jeremiah, others did to Daniel. The Synoptic 'apocalypse' of Mark 13 and its parallels are the best-known example of such reapplication (Matthew showing the closest dependence on the text of Daniel). The Christian Church subsequently applied Daniel's 'prophecies' of the 'son of man', the 'holy ones' (or 'saints'), and the fourth kingdom to Jesus, his Church and Rome respectively, except for the Syrian Church, which maintained a purely historical exegesis. It was almost certainly from a Syrian Christian tradition that the famous, or infamous, anti-Christian writer, Porphyry in the third century derived much of his exegesis of the book. Since Porphyry's arguments evoked a number of detailed responses from Church Fathers, and since his views are nowadays on the whole accepted as critical orthodoxy, he deserves attention. Although his works were burned, the commentary of Jerome (written in AD 407) preserves a good deal of his argumentation.

In fact, Porphyry's conclusions are not exactly as many modern critics represent them to have been. He believed that the whole of Daniel, including ch. 12, was written after the events, and concluded with the success of the Maccabees against Antiochus and his forces; the 'stone' of ch. 2 and the 'Son of Man' of ch. 7 were also representations of the victorious Jewish people. The book was, he argued, pseudo-prophecy, and written to give consolation to the Jews, but in a time later than that of Antiochus. Yet Porphyry does not ascribe any factual errors to Daniel, accepting even the now discredited Darius the Mede. But he identified the four kingdoms of Daniel as the Babylonian, Medo-Persian, Macedonian (Alexander the Great) and finally that of Alexander's successors. With the substitution of Rome as the last empire, this is the traditional and the modern conservative interpretation, not the modern critical one. Porphyry also believed that Daniel had been written in Greek and not Hebrew and Aramaic. He is nevertheless to be credited with establishing the view that the book is a pseudepigraphon, a work written by one author in the name (partly, at least) of another, and he was undoubtedly familiar—as we are now, but the Church Fathers perhaps were not—with several other examples of this device in Jewish literature.

While a prophetic interpretation of Daniel prevailed in Chistendom, Jewish exegesis—not as monolithic as the Christian—tended to distinguish between the wise man Daniel and the prophets, among whom he was *not* reckoned. We also find little messianic interpretation, a feature consistent with a tendency in rabbinic and most mediaeval Jewish interpretation to play down nationalistic messianism. By contrast, Daniel was found well suited in Christendom for political moralizing in the context of the debate about the relationship of Church and State in the Middle Ages, which was taken up also by the Reformers. Calvin used his *Commentaries on Daniel* to defend harassed French Protestants against royal power. With reference to Daniel and Darius (ch. 6), this opponent of royal power wrote in his Thirtieth Lecture:

> We know how earthly empires are constituted by God, only on the condition that he deprives himself of nothing but shines forth alone, and all magistrates must be set in regular order, and every authority in existence must be subject to his glory... earthly princes lay aside all their power when they rise up against God.

In the seventeenth and eighteenth centuries, the criticisms of Porphyry were renewed in the context of the rise of biblical criticism by English Deism and German rationalism. This period also saw the rediscovery of many pseudepigraphic and apocalyptic Jewish and Christian writings, which illuminated the literary context into which a pseudepigraphic Daniel could be set. The crisis of biblical authority in nineteenth-century England, associated with, but not caused by, Darwin's *On the Origin of Species*, set Daniel at the forefront of the issue. As Pusey saw it, Daniel 'admits of no half-measures. It is either divine or an imposture' (p. 75).

S.R. Driver's essay on Daniel at the end of the last century has been seen by many subsequent critics as firmly establishing the modern critical view that Daniel is not a genuine sixth-century prophecy but a second-century pseudepigraph. Conservative reaction to this view has never been lacking, but the thrust of its attack is always to place a burden of irrefutable proof on the backs of those who accept what it often calls the 'critical' position, with a generous use of arguments from silence and the equation of certain possibilities with proven conclusions: thus, if Daniel could even conceivably have been written in the sixth century, then we may legitimately hold that it was, while irrefutable proof is required of any alternative hypothesis.

It would be trivial to deal with such protests, or their logic, here. But with the important essay of Hölscher in 1919 the question of Daniel's literary unity was brought into the discussion, where it still occupies an important place: one of the implications of this is that the question of dating is not a simple alternative between two points of time for the entire contents. Research on apocalyptic, a topic which has revived since the Second World War, has sought, among other things, to relate Daniel to other contemporary and near-contemporary writings, and to explore the origins and history of apocalyptic ideas. While some scholars still regard Daniel as the definitive apocalypse, or at least the earliest one, this view is increasingly in dispute, and there remains in any case some disagreement about the exact relationship of Daniel to other apocalyptic literature, about what constitutes apocalyptic, and indeed, about whether all or only part of Daniel is apocalyptic. Further work on the apocalyptic literature and its roots will, by design or accident, shed much light on the formation of Daniel; but simply labelling Daniel as 'apocalyptic' without a good deal of further qualification amounts to explaining the obscure by the even more obscure and creates more problems than it solves.

In one area of study, progress has been particularly disappointing. Brevard Childs is entirely justified in his verdict that despite a recent spate of books and articles on Daniel, 'it remains a perplexing phenomenon that the theological insights into the book of Daniel have not increased proportionately' (*Introduction to the Old Testament as Scripture*, Philadelphia/London, 1979, p. 613). In the light of current trends in biblical scholarship, the remedy for this deficiency is probably to be sought in a greater appreciation of the *literary* qualities of Daniel, beginning with the recognition that it is a unique composition, and one of the most remarkable within the Bible.

Further Reading

On the 'Additions' to Daniel:

C.A. Moore, *Daniel, Esther and Jeremiah: The Additions* (Anchor Bible), New York: Doubleday, 1977.

On the history of research on Daniel, there are two surveys in German:

W. Baumgartner, 'Ein Vierteljahrhundert Danielforschung', *Theologische Rundschau* 11 (1939), pp. 59-83 [for approximately the first quarter of this century].

J.C.H. Lebram, 'Perspektiven der gegenwärtigen Danielforschung', *JSJ* 5 (1974), pp. 1-33.

A superb guide to the problems of Daniel is also available in German:

K. Koch (and others), *Das Buch Daniel* (Wege der Forschung), Darmstadt: Wissenschaftliche Buchgesellschaft, 1980.

A brief but well-documented account of the history and problems of Daniel research in English is:

*Brevard S. Childs, *An Introduction to the Old Testament as Scripture*, London: SCM / Philadelphia: Fortress, 1979, pp. 608-623.

On Porphyry's critique of Daniel:

P.M. Casey, 'Porphyry and the Origin of the Book of Daniel', *JTS* 27 (1976), pp. 15-33.

The extract from Calvin's Commentaries on Daniel was taken from *On God and Political Duty*, edited by John T. McNeill, Indianapolis: Bobbs-Merrill, 2nd edn, 1956, pp. 101-102.

The following works have been referred to in this chapter by the author's name alone:

S.R. Driver, *An Introduction to the Literature of the Old Testament*, Edinburgh: T. & T. Clark, 9th edn, 1913, ch. 11, substantially reproduced in his *The Book of Daniel (Cambridge Bible for Schools and Colleges), Cambridge: CUP, 1900.

E.B. Pusey, *Daniel, The Prophet*, Oxford: Clarendon Press, 8th edn 1886.

2

THE HISTORICAL BACKGROUND

The two exiles

DANIEL OPENS WITH the capture of Jerusalem and the deportation of Jews to Babylon. According to ch. 1, Daniel entered the service of Nebuchadnezzar and remained active in royal service until the reign of Cyrus. There are problems about the precise dates at either end of Daniel's career; it has been suggested that Daniel's career is intended to cover 70 years exactly, the theologically, if not historically, 'correct' duration. But this can only be a speculation. It is nonetheless fairly certain that Daniel's career is made to coincide more or less exactly with the 'Exile' as understood in biblical history—from 596 until 538 BC.

This understanding of the 'exile' is nevertheless an oversimplification. When Cyrus' edict permitting the Jews to return to Palestine was issued, the majority of Jews did not take advantage of it. The book of Daniel does not mention it. For the majority who remained, the exile obviously did not come to an end. The reasons for their staying in Babylon may have been largely economic or social, but it is probable that some theological justification was also provided. That is to say, the theology of the Second Isaiah whereby God would lead Israel back to its land as he once led them from Egypt was not shared by all exiled Jews (see the volume in this series on *The Second Isaiah* by R.N. Whybray, ch. 5). For some, exile in Babylon was a continuing divine punishment, and the divine displeasure would end only when Israel was properly restored to its land, with the divine blessings fully bestowed and the divine promises fulfilled. In a sense, it could perhaps be said that the exile, for these Jews, would end in the eschaton, the end of the historical process insofar as that process was to be interpreted as the movement from divine promise to fulfilment.

Unfortunately, the Old Testament literature preserves in the main only the tradition and the theology of those Jews who *did* return. These Palestinian Jews have ever since numbered many fewer than their compatriots elsewhere, who formed (and form) the Jewish Diaspora ('dispersion'). We have little direct evidence of the theology of the Babylonian community. But such notions of the Exile are reflected even in the Palestinian sources: on the lips of Ezra we find a recognition that the so-called 'Return' or 'Restoration' was incomplete:

> Behold, we are slaves this day; in the land that thou gavest to our fathers to enjoy its fruit and its good gifts, behold, we are slaves. And its rich yield goes to the kings whom thou hast set over us because of our sins; they have power also over our bodies and over our cattle at their pleasure, and we are in great distress (Nehemiah 9.36-37).

In Daniel, both of these 'exiles' are present. The way they are juxtaposed is a feature of crucial importance for understanding the book of Daniel as a whole. The shorter exile provides the historical context for the career of Daniel, while the longer exile provides the perspective of the visions; but the two notions of exile are brought together in ch. 9, where the exile of seventy years mentioned in Jeremiah is reinterpreted as a span of 'seventy weeks of years', 490 years. It is only at the end of this longer epoch that *true* restoration will take place, and on a more comprehensive scale than the 'restoration' under Cyrus. This will be the culmination of a history in which Jews have lived under a succession of foreign rulers, when a final and eternal kingdom of God's chosen people will be inaugurated.

Moreover, it is from a Palestinian perspective that *both* periods of exile are presented in the book of Daniel as a whole. The longer 'exile' is lived not in geographical exile in Babylonia (or elsewhere) but in the 'glorious land' (11.41), and the succession of kings and kingdoms in chs. 7–12 is presented as it affects Palestine—for example, the struggle over Palestine between the Ptolemaic and Seleucid kingdoms. The shorter exilic period in which Daniel lived is an epoch of the distant past, and the circumstances presented in the stories—loyal service to foreign sovereigns, problems of religious observance in a pagan environment—are not directly applicable to the Jewish community in Palestine. The stories in Daniel are not of Palestinian *origin*, because they clearly reflect a Diaspora, not a Palestinian lifestyle. But by presenting the shorter exile as a prototype, and a metaphor, of the longer exile, Nebuchadnezzar is transformed into Antiochus, and Daniel into the 'Wise' of ch. 12. Indeed, the problems, as well as the answers, addressed in the Daniel stories are transformed.

Since the book of Daniel is, in the sense described, *about* history, then the significance of history, and historical questions, for understanding the argument of the book of Daniel as a whole can hardly be overemphasized. In the light of the above comments we must now consider both the history *of* Daniel and the history *in* Daniel.

From Nebuchadnezzar to Antiochus (c. 600–165 BC)

TABLE I

Chronology of Events from Nebuchadnezzar to Antiochus

Babylonian Empire

587/6	Capture of Jerusalem by Nebuchadnezzar	(Dan. 1.1-4)
	Exile of many Jews	
	Removal of Temple vessels	(5.2)
556	Nabonidus succeeds to throne; later he moves to Arabian desert town of Teima	(cf. ch. 4)
548	Belshazzar becomes ruler in Babylon	(ch. 5)

Persian Empire

539	Cyrus conquers Babylon and becomes ruler	(5.30)
	Belshazzar is killed	
522	Darius I succeeds Cambyses, Cyrus' successor	(6.1, wrongly)
516	Rededication of (second) Temple in Jerusalem	

Greek empire(s)

336–323	Alexander the Great conquers Persian empire	(11.3)
320	Palestine becomes part of the Ptolemaic empire of Egypt	(11.4-5)
198	Antiochus III ('the Great') wins control of Palestine for Seleucids	(11.16)
175	Accession of Antiochus IV (Epiphanes)	(11.21)
167	Cessation of Jewish cult at Temple	(11.31)
164	Rededication of Temple by Judas Maccabee	

Theological considerations apart, a knowledge of the historical context is especially important in the case of Daniel. Such a knowledge must include not just 'bare facts', dates, kings, and so forth, but the accompanying beliefs and attitudes as well. As with all ancient writings, not only does this knowledge help us to understand the contents against their contemporary background, but it also enables us to see where the description in Daniel is at variance with what we believe to have been the true state of affairs. Where this divergence seems unconscious on the part of the author (or authors), a genuine error, we may discover to what extent that author is familiar with the period of which he writes; in the case of deliberate divergence, or exaggeration, we may ask whether the divergence points to a concept whose significance overrides considerations of strict factual accuracy. We shall find instances of both kinds of historical inaccuracy.

The end of the Judean kingdom was brought about by Nebuchadnezzar. He destroyed Jerusalem, plundered the Temple and deported many of the inhabitants. These exiles—representing all but the 'poorest people of the land' (2 Kings 24.15)—settled in villages of their own (Ezek. 3.15), building their own houses, planting vineyards and—according to non-Biblical records from Babylon—setting up in business. Their lack of enthusiasm for a return to their Palestinian home is no doubt largely attributable to their economic and social comfort in the land of 'exile', where they adopted the local language (Aramaic) and used local names, even those including the names of local deities, such as Belteshazzar (Bel), Mordecai (Marduk), or Abed-nego (Nebo?). We know, unfortunately, very little of the religious evolution of these communities, although a great deal can be inferred: biblical scholars have concluded that there was a great deal of literary activity, resulting in the production of law-codes and historiography as well as the editing of prophetic books and the preaching (or writing) of prophets like Ezekiel and the Second Isaiah.

What developments in Jewish ideas did these circumstances induce? Considerable adjustment was needed to a new situation: gone were the Temple and the land, and with them the monarchy, the nation-state, and the formal political rôle of the prophet. Gone was the God who defended his holy city. In brief, the religion of Israelite theologians (at least), built on the concept of God as a warrior king who had chosen his own people, installed them in their own land, and spoken to them through history and in the cult, was in disarray. The most important issue for a student of Daniel to appreciate, however, is the issue of God's control of history. Were not other gods in control of the destiny of Babylon, including its Jewish inhabitants? Both the Second Isaiah and Daniel assert the universal sovereignty of the Jewish God; both ask, how is God's sovereignty still effective? Second Isaiah speaks in terms drawn from Israel's sacred history, and sees the answer in a restoration of nationhood through an act of divine might, unlike Daniel, which takes a view broader both in time and space. Jews had no political influence, and their behaviour could therefore have no direct effect on the course of political events. How could their wickedness any longer bring military defeat or their repentance earn deliverance?

The stories of the book of Daniel reflect the tension between political and religious loyalties, and between individual and national destiny; they come from communities forming a religious and ethnic minority in geographical exile. For Jews who returned to Palestine, different circumstances created different problems: political opposition from Samaria, the establishment of priestly authority, and the constitution of an exclusive community centred on a Temple cultus. Of this community in the Persian period the book of Daniel says nothing. One extremely important outcome of this period, however, is the establishment of both religious and political leadership in the person of the High Priest. Although this state of affairs did not establish itself immediately, it became a cornerstone of the reconstructed Jewish society. The High Priest represented the Jews of Palestine to the Persians: he was both spiritual and secular ruler, and the Temple and the royal palace were symbolically one. The notion of a theocracy, that God was effectively the ruler of Israel, could be plausibly sustained under this arrangement. The work of the Chronicler illustrates how the 'house of David' means no longer the divinely sustained royal dynasty, but the Temple itself—which David had inaugurated.

The advent of Alexander the Great, who devoured the Persian empire in the third quarter of the fourth century BC, marks a significant point in the history and the religion of Palestinian Judaism. Although Hellenistic influence predated the arrival of Greek armies in the region, the untimely death of Alexander in 323 provoked a struggle among his generals for the lands he had conquered. Political sovereignty over the Jews was thereafter a matter to be settled by Gentile kings and their armies, and the dispute for control of Palestine generated internal divisions, some Jews favouring the Seleucid kingdom based in Syria, others the Ptolemaic based in Egypt. Relations between these powers during the third century, alluded to in Daniel 10–11, included many battles and an attempt at treaty by marriage, and ended with Seleucid victory in 199. During this period, but not reflected in Daniel, pro-Ptolemaic and pro-Seleucid factions crystallized among the priestly (Oniad) and aristocratic (Tobiad) families. But, more momentously, divisions had also grown concerning the extent to which the religion of the people of Judah could accommodate Hellenistic ideas and practices. The issue which finally precipitated a crisis was not essentially about Hellenistic culture itself, which had already influenced Judaism considerably, but, it seems, about the intrusion of Hellenism into the system of government by which political and religious authority had been fused—the High Priesthood. The High Priesthood and the Temple were guarantees of the kingship of God over Israel, and their manipulation by a Gentile king was, not unreasonably, open to interpretation as a challenge to God.

Until this crisis, the Jews had been officially permitted by one ruler after another to conduct their own religious affairs under the High Priest. However, under Antiochus IV (Epiphanes), the High Priesthood itself was bought from the king, and as a result certain parties succeeded in establishing within Jerusalem a Hellenistic city with the usual trappings. The political and religious instability of the Jewish community led to revolt, which—aided by the frustration of Antiochus' ambitions in Egypt—provoked a royal decree abolishing the Jewish cult, replacing it by another and forbidding Jewish practices. The Jewish community was therefore assailed both by inner division and by external threat. In chs. 7–12, which originate from this period, it is the external threat which predominates until the end, where the writer, in ch. 12, looks beyond the removal of the wicked 'king of the north' and turns his eye upon the divided Jewish people.

Our knowledge of the historical events of the both the shorter and the longer 'exiles' brings us to two different questions: the time and place of composition of the stories and visions of Daniel and the theological understanding of history and politics which Daniel presents. In the case of Daniel we can separate the two questions fairly neatly, and here we shall consider the former—which has aroused more controversy than any other critical question—as our next topic.

The stories of Daniel and history

TABLE II

Succession of Rulers from Nebuchadnezzar to Darius I

Babylonian			Median	
605/4–562	Nebuchadnezzar			
560	Amel-Marduk			
560–556	Neriglissar			
556–539	Nabonidus	Cyaxares		625–585
(548–539	Belshazzar)	Astyages		585–550

Persian		
539–530	Cyrus	550–530
530–522	Cambyses	
522–486	Darius I (Hystaspes)	

The assumption that Daniel wrote chs. 1–6 of the book bearing his name was for centuries the traditional view, and retains its adherents. There is no logical or natural reason for this view, for while the visions claim to be by Daniel, they are at least written in the first person. By that token, however, Nebuchadnezzar and not Daniel should be taken as the author of ch. 4.

The fact is that the stories might have been written by anyone at any time. That they are intended as historical accounts must be established, not assumed, and an important step in addressing this question is their historical reliability. There are several respects in which this reliability has been questioned:

i. There is no such historical character as 'Darius the Mede'.

ii. There was no Median empire between the Babylonian and Persian.

iii. The conquest of Jerusalem by Nebuchadnezzar is incorrectly dated.

iv. Belshazzar was not king of Babylon, nor was he a son of Nebuchadnezzar.

v. There were no attempts by rulers of Babylon to impose cults on its citizens.

i. *Darius the Mede*

According to 5.30 'Darius the Mede' received the kingdom from Belshazzar the 'Chaldean king', being 62 years old. 'Darius' is a Persian name, borne by several monarchs: Darius I (Hystaspes) succeeded Cambyses in 522, Darius II succeeded Xerxes (= 'Ahasuerus' in Hebrew) in 423 and Darius III, who came to the throne in 336, was the last, being defeated by Alexander the Great. The notice in 9.1 that Darius the Mede was the 'son of Ahasuerus' (Xerxes) implies a confusion, and the addition of the words 'by birth a Mede', perhaps acknowledges the dilemma. It seems that at least two Persian monarchs have been confused, and a fictitious third created out of the confusion. Darius I is indicated by the statement in 6.1 that Darius established 120 satrapies throughout the kingdom. Such a system of administration is indisputably Persian, not Median; and according to Esther Ahasuerus (Xerxes) had 127 satrapies. Darius II was the only Darius whose predecessor was Xerxes. Those unwilling to accept explanations involving historical error on the part of Daniel have usually opted to select or invent an historical person who might been conceived as having succeeded Belshazzar and to try to put upon him the name 'Darius'. The three most common candidates are Cambyses, Gobryas and Astyages. Cambyses was actually Cyrus' successor, but he is thought to qualify as predecessor on the ground that he bore the title 'king' during Cyrus' reign. Gobryas (Gubaru or Ugbaru), according to the *Nabonidus Chronicle* and the Greek adventurer and writer Xenophon (who campaigned in Persia) actually captured Babylon from Belshazzar, and historically is the only plausible predecessor of Cyrus as ruler of Babylon; but, as Rowley in a definitive treatment has spelt out, there is no evidence that he was called Darius, was a son of Ahasuerus, was a Mede or was called king. Astyages was a Median king at whose court Cyrus apparently spent time. But there is no record that Astyages ever went to Babylon, much less ruled over it. (Josephus, incidentally, made Darius the *son* of Astyages, possibly in an effort to rescue Daniel from error.)

A fourth, and at first sight plausible, candidate is Cyaxares II, whom Xenophon names as Astyages' son. But the existence of such a ruler is unconfirmed by Babylonian sources, and Xenophon's account is in any case highly unreliable. The testimony of all contemporary sources agrees that it was Cyrus who succeeded the last Babylonian king as ruler of Babylon, and there is no place for any other figure, whether or not called Darius. With this verdict we come to the question of the Median empire.

ii. *The kingdom of the Medes*

In chs. 2 and 7 a scheme is projected of four world-empires preceding the final and permanent kingdom, of which the first is the (neo-) Babylonian whose most notable monarch was Nebuchadnezzar. Early Christian interpretation, understandably, took the final kingdom of Daniel to be that established by Christ, and accordingly found in the fourth empire Rome. (Indeed, the Synoptic 'apocalypses' [Mark 13; Matthew 24; Luke 21] clearly have the same understanding.) If Rome is the fourth, then the Median kingdom becomes an embarrassing supernumerary. Accordingly it is as a rule taken with the Persian to form a joint Medo-Persian kingdom.

It has been argued, accordingly, that this is precisely how Daniel presents the second empire of the scheme. In 8.20 a single beast with two horns represents the 'kings of Media and Persia'. The book of Esther, too, regularly associates Medes and Persians, referring to 'the army chiefs of Persia and Media' (1.3), 'ladies of Persia and Media' (1.18) and 'laws of the Persians and the Medes' (1.19). While Esther apparently assumes the order of importance, however, Daniel employs the correct chronological sequence in placing Medes before Persians throughout. The combination of Media and Persia is historically justifiable: Cyrus inherited by conquest the Median kingdom which he then united with the Persian (see Table II).

Yet this explanation does not settle the problem. That 8.20 does represent the two kingdoms by a single animal does not necessarily mean they are seen as a single empire, particularly since in 10.1 Cyrus is called 'king of Persia' and not 'king of the Medes and Persians'. And from the historical point of view it is equally correct to speak of a Median kingdom existing before Cyrus incorporated it into his Persian empire. And although Esther associates Medes and Persians, Isaiah 13.17, 21.2 and Jeremiah 51.11 attribute the destruction of Babylon to the Medes—quite inaccurately, for the Medes at no time conquered or ruled Babylon. Since the evidence is generally ambiguous, considerable weight must attach to Daniel's description of the fourth kingdom. What is said of the fourth kingdom in Daniel can be made to fit Rome only with intransigent and perverse exegesis: 8.21ff. in particular makes it as clear as is necessary that the final wicked ruler belongs to the kingdom of the Greeks, for v. 21

names the 'king of Greece', from whom, according to the vision (v. 9) the 'little horn' grew. This 'little horn' is the final aggressor, the king mentioned in v. 23. There is simply nowhere for a further kingdom to be found. The details of the fourth kingdom in ch. 11 also reflect plausibly the history of the Greek kingdoms, while the 'ships of Kittim' in 11.30 are the Romans. Again, there is no statement to the effect that another kingdom supersedes before the final divine intervention.

Since the fourth kingdom is, on the evidence of Daniel itself, that of the Greeks, the successors of Alexander the Great, the first three must be Babylon, Media and Persia. As we have already seen, this is not an historically fictitious sequence, although Daniel is incorrect in having its hero subject to a Median king, for the Medes were never sovereigns of Babylonia.

At this point it is helpful to point out that a scheme of successive world-empires may be an ancient one, inherited, along with the total of four, by Daniel. From a different perspective—e.g. Asia Minor, the sequence Media–Persia–Greece would be entirely plausible. That Daniel has adopted such a scheme from elsewhere is quite probable, but not certain. But it may be that here, as in other cases to be discussed, the historical knowledge of Daniel is not derived from first-hand knowledge, but borrowed from other sources. In this case, it is tempting to suggest that Daniel 8.30-31, reporting the punishment of Belshazzar's profane, even idolatrous, use of Temple vessels is inspired by Jeremiah 51.12:

> The LORD has stirred up the spirit of the kings of the Medes, because his purpose concerning Babylon is to destroy it, for that is the vengeance of the LORD, the vengeance for his temple.

iii. *The conquest of Jerusalem*
Daniel 1.1ff. states:

> In the third year of the reign of Jehoiakim king of Judah, Nebuchadnezzar king of Babylon came to Jerusalem and besieged it. And the LORD gave Jehoiakim king of Judah into his hand, with some of the vessels of the house of God... Then the king commanded... to bring some of the people of Israel, both of the royal family and of the nobility... to serve in the king's palace.

There are all sorts of problems here. First, the account of 2 Kings 24 and the contemporary Babylonian sources are essentially in agreement over the course of events leading to the Judean exile. 2 Kings 24.1f. reads:

> Nebuchadnezzar king of Babylon came up, and Jehoiakim became his servant three years; then he turned and rebelled against him. And the LORD sent against him bands of the Chaldeans . . . and sent them against Judah to destroy it.

However, no capture of the city is recorded; Jehoiakim 'slept with his fathers' (v. 6) and Jerusalem was actually attacked by Nebuchadnezzar after Jehoiachin had been on the throne for three months (v. 10). It is now generally assumed that Jehoiakim died before the reprisal which he had provoked materialized, leaving his son to face Nebuchadnezzar. 2 Chronicles 36.6f. however, goes further:

> Against him [Jehoiakim] came up Nebuchadnezzar king of Babylon, and bound him in fetters to take him to Babylon. Nebuchadnezzar also carried part of the vessels of the house of the   LORD to Babylon.

Some commentators have taken the Chronicles account as confirming Daniel 1.1. But this argument again cuts both ways, for Daniel might be held to be dependent on Chronicles rather than historical fact. Indeed, if scripture rather than history is Daniel's source, the 'third year' of Daniel 1.1 might be traced back to the 'three years' of 2 Kings 24. As with the Medes, therefore, it is a reasonable suggestion that Daniel derives its information indirectly, in this case, by a conflation of texts from scripture. In actual fact, the third year of Jehoiakim was 606, before Nebuchadnezzar was 'king of Babylon'. It was also the year in which he conquered the Pharaoh Necho at Carchemish, and a siege of Jerusalem at this time is improbable. However, the dating of the story of Daniel 1 to the *second* year of Nebuchadnezzar is an even more puzzling contradiction which suggests that the chronological notices of the book were not intended, and should not therefore be taken, too literally.

iv. *Belshazzar*

Critical commentaries, especially around the turn of the century, made much of the fact that Belshazzar was neither a son of Nebuchadnezzar nor king of Babylon. This is still sometimes repeated as a charge against the historicity of Daniel, and resisted by conservative scholars. But it has been clear since 1924 (Montgomery, pp. 66-67) that although Nabonidus was the last king of the neo-Babylonian dynasty, Belshazzar was effectively ruling Babylon. In this respect, then, Daniel is correct. The literal meaning of 'son' should not be pressed; even if it might betray a misunderstanding on the part of Daniel, a strong case against Daniel's historical reliability is not enhanced by the inclusion of weak arguments such as this.

v. *Religious intolerance in Babylon*

There is no evidence of successive attempts by any of the kings mentioned in the stories of Daniel to enforce observance of a particular cult. Nor is there any evidence of the conversion of any of the kings (even once!) to worship of the Jewish God. These are not mere arguments from silence, for in the case of persecution the historically attested reluctance of Jews to leave Babylon (while remaining religiously as well as ethnically Jewish) suggests tolerance of their religion, while in the case of royal conversion, there is not the slightest trace in any historical source either of a change of religious allegiance or of any decree or policy attributable to such a change, an absence which is surely significant.

The fact is, of course, that the discrepancy between historical fact and the Danielic stories is of such a scale as to make the squabbling over individual points of error rather trivial, and to remind readers who want to hear the message of the book not to insist on their own dogmatic rules. The picture painted in the stories of life in sixth-century exile was obviously good enough for its original readers, whom, we must conclude, were not themselves living at that time (nor, it follows, were the authors). The question of date and setting cannot really be decided on the kinds of issue we have so far discussed. Indeed, whether there is 'a date' begs an important question about the composition of the stories, while the question of setting (and function) is best answered by analysing the genre and plot of the stories themselves. This will concern us in a later chapter.

The visions of Daniel and history
(see Table III)

From what has been said already, it will be evident that the visions of chs. 7–12 betray a close acquaintance with the political history of the Greek kingdoms in the neighbourhood of Palestine. While knowledge of the Medes and Persians seems to be a little shaky, the amount of

TABLE III:
CHRONOLOGICAL CHART IN DETAIL OF
EVENTS FROM ALEXANDER TO ANTIOCHUS

Events from Alexander to Antiochus
IV Reflected in Daniel 11

334–333	Victories of Alexander the Great over Darius III at the Granicus and at Issus	(11.3)
320–198	Palestine belongs to the Ptolemaic empire of Egypt	(11.4-5)
261–246	Reign of the Seleucid king Antiochus II; he marries the Ptolemaic princess Berenice	(11.6)
246–226	Hostilities between Seleucus II and Ptolemy III over control of Palestine	(11.7-9)
223–187	Reign of Antiochus III ('the Great'); he wins control of Palestine in 198;	(11.11-17)
	marries his daughter to Ptolemy V	(11.17b)
	defeated by Romans at Magnesia in 189	(11.18)
175	Accession of Antiochus III (Epiphanes)	(11.21ff.)
168	Antiochus invades Egypt but is turned back by Roman legate	(11.29-30)
167	Cessation of the daily burnt offering and erection of new altar	(11.31)
	Maccabean resistance	(11.32) (?)
165	Rededication of altar by Judas Maccabee	

informed detail increases towards the reign of Antiochus IV. Table III shows possible allusions to events in Daniel; most scholars believe that such references are intended to be clear to the original readers. But we cannot be completely certain of all our identifications.

It is natural, of course, that as the anticipated climax of history approaches, so will the detail of description. But there is no denying two simple observations: that as time progresses, the book of Daniel becomes more detailed and (apparently) more accurate; and yet that at a precise point in its charting of the course of history the book *departs* from what we know to have happened. This point, according to most scholars, occurs at 11.40, where the genuine prediction is perhaps deliberately marked by the formula 'at the time of the end'. The war between the 'king of the south' and the 'king of the north'—presumably Antiochus of Syria and Ptolemy of Egypt—which brings the latter into Palestine and to his death did not take place, although Antiochus did confront Egypt. The slaughter in the 'glorious land' did not occur, nor was Egypt itself conquered. Indeed, it is unlikely that Antiochus would have attempted any such conquest, since the powerful Romans had already forbidden such aggression on pain of war. Certainly, Antiochus did not become ruler of Egypt. Whether the prediction of 11.40ff. was based on political calculation or on particular biblical prophecies, it did not come to pass. Antiochus died not in Palestine but in Parthia; there was no manifestation of the archangel Michael and no resurrection; while the Jewish kingdom, won by the human agency of Maccabean warriors and preserved by Hasmonean priest-kings, lasted but a century.

The presence of genuine prediction in Daniel, betrayed by its subsequent *deviation* from the actual course of events, means none-theless that the visions are among the most precisely datable parts of the Old Testament literature. They all betray a knowledge of the abolition of the *Tamid* sacrifice, which was a regular twice-daily burnt offering, performed in the morning and at dusk, unlike sacrifices offered on festivals or by individuals on specified occasions. Daniel knows of the interruption of this daily service by Antiochus, which occurred in 167 BC, but not of the circumstances of the death of Antiochus, which happened in 164 BC. This is not to say, of course, that all even of chs. 7–12 were written in this period, for there is plentiful evidence of revision within this material (the different calculations of the time of the end in ch. 12 being an obvious example). We can say, however, that not only the series of visions,

but the book of Daniel in its canonical form was produced during the
persecution of Antiochus IV.

Further Reading

For the historical background:

> H.H. Rowley, *Darius the Mede and the Four World Empires of
> Daniel*, Cardiff: University Press of Wales, 1935 (reprinted 1959).

> *D.S. Russell, *The Jews from Alexander the Great to Herod* (New
> Clarendon Bible), Oxford: OUP, 1967, pp. 1-59.

> W.D. Davies and L. Finkelstein (eds.), *The Cambridge History of
> Judaism*, I, Cambridge: CUP, 1984, pp. 70-87; 130-61 (Palestine)
> and 326-58 (Babylonian Diaspora) [Bibliographies are given on
> pp. 401-46].

> J.H. Hayes and J.M. Miller (eds.), *Israelite and Judaean History*
> (OTL), London: SCM Press / Philadelphia: Westminster Press,
> 1977, pp. 480-86 (the Jews in Babylonia), 489-578 (the Persian
> period) and 568-85 (the Hellenistic period). [All these sections have
> bibliographies].

On the theology of exilic and post-exilic Judaism:

> P.R. Ackroyd, *Exile and Resoration (OTL)*, London: SCM Press/
> Philadelphia: Westminster Press, 1968.

> *J.M. Myers, *The World of the Restoration*, Englewood Cliffs:
> Prentice-Hall, 1968.

> *R.N. Whybray, *The Second Isaiah* (Old Testament Guides),
> Sheffield: JSOT Press, 1983.

A translation of the *Nabonidus Chronicle* is given in *ANET*, pp. 305-
306.

3

THE LANGUAGES
OF THE BOOK

The bilingual problem

THE PRESENCE, and the distribution, of the two languages in Daniel may be in the end inexplicable. But it has generally been thought to have a bearing on the literary history or structure of the book. The evaluation of this phenomenon depends on whether or not the literary unity of Daniel is taken for granted. An ancient view, for instance, holds that Daniel composed in Hebrew those parts of his book written for his compatriots, and in Aramaic those parts intended for Gentile readers. Among modern commentators many conservative scholars take a similar view, as do some of those who maintain a second-century date for the whole book, such as Otto Plöger and H.H. Rowley; the latter has argued that the author first issued stories (chs. 2–7) in Aramaic for the encouragement of his compatriots, and later added the visions (chs. 8–12) in Hebrew for a more learned audience, binding the two together with a Hebrew introduction (1.1–2.4) which replaced the original Aramaic one. This view is also favoured by Porteous, Delcor and others. Nevertheless, it remains curious on this view that the Hebrew should change to Aramaic at 2.4. Here we read: 'Then the Chaldeans said to the king in Aramaic . . . ', and what follows *is* in Aramaic!

S.R. Driver suggested that the author began in Hebrew and switched to Aramaic when reporting direct speech in that language. Now, in Ezra 4.8-23, 5.1–6.18 and 7.12-26 official correspondence is quoted in Aramaic. Indeed, in Ezra 6 the Aramaic overruns the source for several verses. However, in Daniel the overrun extends for six chapters, and Driver's explanation, that the author forgot to revert to Hebrew, is not very convincing. Indeed, we now know that the phrase 'in Aramaic' is absent from Qumran fragments of Daniel (which are the earliest manuscripts we have of the book). Instead, there is a space, presumably to draw attention to the change of language at this point. Accordingly, many modern commentators suspect the phrase is a scribal note serving the same purpose.

Another set of solutions becomes available if one presumes that the book was written, whether by one or several authors, originally in one language only. A.A. Bevan surmised that part of the Hebrew original had been lost and was replaced by an Aramaic version. A much more popular view, offered by R.H. Charles, is that Daniel was composed in Aramaic. This proposal has more recently been argued forcefully by H.L. Ginsberg, and is based essentially on the poor quality of the Hebrew and on a number of instances where the Hebrew is explicable only, or better, as a translation from Aramaic. Not all scholars are convinced by Ginsberg's examples, and his argument is made less attractive because it forms part of a complicated reconstruction of the literary history in many stages. Ginsberg's explanation for the partial translation from Aramaic to Hebrew was that it was made to ensure that the book, by beginning and ending in Hebrew, would receive canonical recognition. This explanation (along with Ginsberg's entire thesis) is accepted by Hartman and Di Lella, but Lacocque, while accepting the theory of translation into Hebrew, mocks the proposed explanation: 'as though the "inspectors" or customs officials would content themselves with a cursory examination of the merchandise' (p. 14).

The presumption of multiple authorship of the book affords yet more possible explanations. The simplest application of this proposal is that one author wrote in Aramaic and a second added chapters in Hebrew, ch. 1 being composed or translated by the second author, or perhaps by a third. This was the suggestion of C.C. Torrey, which also attracted J.A. Montgomery. However, the strongest evidence for multiple authorship consists in the difference of genre and theology between the stories (chs. 1–6) and the visions (chs. 7–12), and this very distinction cuts right across the language division, since ch. 7 belongs generically with the other visions in 8–12 but linguistically with chs. 2–6. Possibly ch. 7 is the product of some intermediate stage in the literary history of Daniel; some scholars (e.g. Noth, Lenglet) believe that it once formed a conclusion to a collection of stories before the other visions were added. Another explanation sees its ambivalence, as being on the one hand a vision yet on the other hand written in Aramaic, in terms of a redactional device intended to weld together the two parts of the book (Collins).

All of the explanations of the bilingualism mentioned are possible, but they cannot be evaluated in isolation from other considerations regarding the literary structure and history of Daniel. The phenomenon is capable of too many explanations to provide on its own any kind of working hypothesis. In the end, the bilingual phenomenon will have to be explained in a way which fits in best with other evidence about the structure and history of Daniel. It cannot form the starting point for an analysis of the book's composition.

Dating the languages

Aramaic, the language of Daniel 2–7, was spoken during many centuries and at times over the entire Middle East. Only in this century, however, has it become possible to attempt to identify the date and provenance of Daniel on the basis of the Aramaic dialect it uses; and the results, if not conclusive, are interesting. At the end of the last century, the corpus of Aramaic literature available was rather small: the 'biblical Aramaic' in Ezra and Daniel, the Jewish Targums (from a later period altogether) and inscriptions and texts from beyond the Euphrates. Accordingly, Aramaic was at first rather simply classified into 'western' and 'eastern' forms. 'Biblical Aramaic' was deemed to be 'western'. This verdict was naturally seized upon by champions of the second-century date. In the words of Driver: 'the Aramaic of Daniel . . . is a *western* Aramaic dialect, of the type spoken in and about *Palestine*' (*The Book of Daniel*, p. lix). Rowley fervently advocated the same view. However, further discoveries of Aramaic texts, such as the Jewish archives from Elephantine in Egypt (early postexilic period) threw doubt upon the simplistic distinctions in vogue; and a development of fundamental importance was the identification of an Aramaic dialect which had been adopted officially by the Persian chancellery. It was dubbed 'Imperial Aramaic' (*Reichsaramäisch*) or Official Aramaic, and it had been in use from the sixth century BC until the end of the third. This discovery appeared to invalidate the distinction between eastern and western Aramaic dialects during the centuries in question. Imperial Aramaic was essentially an eastern dialect, and it is now generally acknowledged as the dialect of Biblical Aramaic not only of Daniel, but also of the other specimen of Biblical Aramaic in Ezra, and the Elephantine papyri from Egypt. This being so, it is not possible in the present state of research to determine the geographical provenance of a text in Imperial Aramaic.

Nevertheless, some argument is possible on the question of dating the Aramaic portion of Daniel. Advocates of a second-century date for the whole book are able to point to the presence of Persian and Greek words which, they argue, rule out a sixth-century date for its composition. The Greek words, are, admittedly, confined to technical musical terms, and it has been objected that such these terms, as well as Persian words, might have been available to a sixth-century Jew. But the balance of probability weighs heavily against this argument. Perhaps the most important evidence, linguistically, against such a date is the use of the word 'Chaldean' to mean a class of magician in ten of its twelve occurrences in Daniel. Such a usage hardly belongs to the sixth century, when the term was a racial one, denoting the Babylonians. This is its meaning in Kings, Isaiah, Jeremiah, Ezekiel, Habakkuk and twice in Daniel, at 5.30 and 9.1. This kind of consideration leads to the conclusion that the Aramaic portions of Daniel are not the product of a Babylonian Jew under Nebuchadnezzar or his immediate successors.

The Jews deported to Babylonia obviously spoke Hebrew as a first language, and we have a reasonable amount of biblical material from this period. After the return, fluency in Hebrew is certainly less widespread. It appears from Nehemiah 8.8 that the law had to be translated into Aramaic for the people. Yet Ezra, Nehemiah and Chronicles, as well as other biblical books, attest the continuing use of Hebrew as a literary, and almost certainly also a spoken, tongue in Palestine. But even when authors of this period attempt a classical style (Jonah and Esther being good examples) features such as changes in the use of individual words, the structure of clauses and the use of tenses identify what is now commonly referred to as 'Late Biblical Hebrew'. The Hebrew of Daniel is certainly not the Hebrew of a sixth-century Jewish exile. It reads like the language of one not fluent in Hebrew, one whose first language was Aramaic. But the quality of Hebrew represented by, let us say, Esther, Ben Sira and the Qumran Scrolls is so varied that no more precise dating of Daniel's Hebrew is possible. One may only comment that if the authors of the visions were scribes, as is widely believed, their standard of Hebrew is surprisingly poor (much worse than Ben Sira's, a scribe of the early second century BC), and Ginsberg's suggestion that it is a translation must remain a firm possibility, whether or not (as we have warned) this conclusion creates other difficulties.

Further Reading

On the bilingualism of Daniel:

C.C. Torrey, 'Notes on the Aramaic Part of Daniel', *Transactions of the Connecticut Academy of Arts and Sciences* 15 (1909), pp. 241-82.

H.H. Rowley, 'The Bilingual Problem of Daniel', *ZAW* 50 (1932), pp. 256-68.

H.L. Ginsberg, *Studies in Daniel*, New York: Jewish Theological Seminary, 1948.

*H.H. Rowley, 'The Unity of the Book of Daniel', in *The Servant of the Lord and Other Essays on the Old Testament*, Oxford: Blackwell, 2nd edn, 1965, pp. 249-80. This is in large measure a reply to Ginsberg.

H.L. Ginsberg, 'The Composition of the Book of Daniel', *VT* 4 (1954), pp. 246-75: a response to Rowley.

On Aramaic and Hebrew in the Persian period:

*J. Naveh and J. Greenfield, 'Hebrew and Aramaic in the Persian Period', in *The Cambridge History of Judaism*, pp. 115-29 (and bibliography, 421-25).

*E. Kutscher, 'Aramaic', in *Encyclopaedia Judaica*, III, pp. 259-87.

E. Kutscher, *A History of the Hebrew Language*, Jerusalem: Magnes Press / Leiden: Brill, 1982.

Other works referred to:

*A.A. Bevan, *A Short Commentary on the Book of Daniel*, Cambridge: CUP, 1882.

*R.H. Charles, *A Critical and Exegetical Commentary on the Book of Daniel*, Oxford: Clarendon Press, 1929.

4

THE STORY CYCLE

The figure of Daniel

ACCORDING TO ch. 1, Daniel was a Jewish noble deported to Babylon near the beginning of the sixth century BC. Since he survived until the reign of Cyrus (1.21; 10.1) he lived at least until about 538 BC. Nothing else about this Daniel is told outside the biblical book (apart from the deuterocanonical stories). Ezra 8.12 and Nehemiah 10.7 mention a Daniel among lists of returned captives, but these references are too late, tempting as they have been to a few commentators. Ezekiel makes three references to a Daniel. In 14.14, 20 he appears with Noah and Job who are given as examples of righteous men. It has been pointed out that Noah and Job are both figures of great antiquity, and indeed neither is Jewish (the covenant with Noah was seen in Jewish tradition as binding on all mankind); our Daniel is an improbable companion to these. In 8.23 Ezekiel sarcastically addresses the king of Tyre thus: 'You are indeed wiser than Daniel'. Here it seems that a figure of some renown, known also to the king of Tyre, must be intended, or else the jibe loses its effect. Other considerations are that the name 'Daniel' is spelled slightly differently in Ezekiel and that our Daniel may not have acquired such a great reputation by the time of Ezekiel's remarks.

It has therefore been concluded that another 'Daniel' or perhaps 'Dan'el' must have been widely known as a wise and righteous figure in Ezekiel's time. Several scholars have drawn attention to a king called Dan'el in the Ugaritic texts, a righteous ruler of human or semi-divine proportions, the father of Aqhat. According to *Aqhat* II.v. 7-8 (see *ANET*, pp. 149-55) he 'judges the cause of the widow, tries the case of the orphan'.

Two other figures may briefly be noted: in the book of Jubilees (written in the second century BC, but perhaps containing more ancient traditions) Dan'el is the father-in-law (and possibly uncle too) of the archetypal Jewish wise man, Enoch (4.20). In 1 Enoch 6.7 (third or second century BC) Dan'el appears as one of the angelic leaders who brought two hundred of the 'sons of heaven' to earth to teach 'charms and enchantments' to men, a version of the story preserved in Genesis 6.1-6; although a wicked figure, he has been identified by one scholar with the Dan(i)el of Ezekiel. There may well be a kind of relationship between some of these figures, but none of these other texts throws direct light on our exilic hero.

A more helpful clue lies in a text from Qumran. In the so-called 'Nabonidus fragment' (4QPrNab), the Babylonian king relates how he had prayed to 'gods of silver and gold . . . wood and stone and clay' but was healed of an evil ulcer which had afflicted him for seven years in Teiman by an exorcist 'who was a Jew'. Parallels with Daniel 4 are obvious: the king speaks in the first person; he is afflicted for seven years, he worships idols; he has an encounter with a Jew.

The differences, however, are also interesting. First, the story is told of Nabonidus, the last king of Babylon, who did live at Teima in the Arabian desert, leaving his kingdom in the hands of Belshazzar. This we know from Babylonian texts. For example the *Nabonidus Chronicle* reports: 'Ninth year: Nabonidus the king (stayed) in Tema; the crown prince, the officials and the army (were) in Akkad. The king did not come to Babylon for the (ceremony of the) month of Nisanu . . . ' An identical entry follows for the tenth year (see *ANET*, p. 306). The 'crown prince' referred to is Belshazzar, as, for example, a tablet in the Yale Babylonian Collection shows: 'I have observed the Great Star and I shall study (this) with regard to a favourable interpretation for my lord Nabonidus, king of Babylon, as well as to my lord Belshazzar, the crown-prince!' (*ANET*, pp. 309f. n. 5).

A second difference is that the Jew whom Nabonidus met was unnamed, and healed him. The circumstances fit the suggestion that the Qumran text is a more original form of the story that we have in Daniel 4, and indeed the biblical story acquires a new aspect when seen in the light of it. Historically, the dwelling in Teima(n) fits Nabonidus, and even the fate of Nebuchadnezzar, whose dwelling was to be with the beasts of the field, eating grass like an ox (4.25), is a plausible description of that king's lifestyle, at least to disaffected Babylonian citizens.

The biblical story, then, exhibits three significant changes from the Qumran version: it has altered the monarch from the little known

Nabonidus to the better-known arch-enemy of the Jews, Nebuchadnezzar; it has given the unknown Jew the name of Daniel; and it has
changed the story from a healing into a foretelling. All three respects
are best explained as the result of the story's being drawn into a
'Daniel cycle'.

If such a process is true in the case of ch. 4, can we detect
elsewhere in chs. 1–6 a process whereby traditional material about
other heroes has been attached to Daniel? Such a development is
suggested by the stories about Shadrach, Meshach and Abednego
(ch. 3), and the appearance of Belteshazzar in chs. 2, 4 and 5. In ch. 1
these Babylonian names are given to the three Jewish friends of
Daniel, while the name Belteshazzar is given to Daniel himself. The
use of the Babylonian names thereafter, with occasional reminders of
the Jewish names, is very difficult to account for except on the
assumption that stories about Belteshazzar have been attached to
Daniel, and three heroes of another story have been made into
friends of Daniel. The alternative name for Daniel is thus a necessary
device; in the case of the three, the Hebrew names may have been
provided because, having been identified as companions of Daniel,
they were entitled to both Jewish and Babylonian names as well.
Accordingly, most of the stories in Daniel 1–6 did not originate as
Daniel stories at all.

Our examination of the figure of Daniel, then, has shifted focus
from the historical character to the legendary hero. We cannot say
for certain whether Daniel was recognized as a major Jewish hero
before the book bearing his name appeared. But Ben Sira, writing not
long before the crisis which produced the book of Daniel makes no
mention of him in his review of great figures of the past (Ecclus 44–
50). The origins of this hero, wherever they are to be found, lie
outside the Old Testament. Our attention must now be directed
more closely to the formation of the Daniel cycle. We shall consider
first the question of the redaction (i.e. the final editing) of the cycle,
and then by an analysis of ch. 2 illustrate the history of one of the
stories from its earliest discernible stages to its present form.

Redaction of the cycle

A framework for the stories is provided by ch. 1 and also by a number
of notices at the beginnings and endings of chapters; there is also an
ideological framework in the notion of a series of world-kingdoms
represented by successive monarchs served by Daniel.

Chapter 1

There is some difference of opinion as to whether ch. 1 is an original self-contained story, or was composed specifically as an introduction to the tales. If, however, the stories of Daniel originated independently, as has been suggested earlier, ch. 1 must have been supplied or adapted to provide a common framework for them. It is this chapter which explains how Daniel and his companions came to be in Babylon, how they came to be counted among the wise men at the royal court, how they acquired Babylonian names, how Daniel exhibited 'understanding in all visions and dreams' and how he also 'continued until the first year of King Cyrus'. This chapter therefore anticipates and embraces all of the following tales. Some scholars have seen it as an introduction to the entire book, but its description of Daniel as an interpreter of visions and dreams but not as a recipient of them seems to confine its portrait to the contents of chs. 1–6 only. Moreover, ch. 10.1 is dated to the *third* year of Cyrus.

There are some discrepancies between chs. 1 and 2 which are best explained on the assumption that ch. 2 was not written by the author of ch. 1, but existed already, and has been only partly harmonized (see below).

Other notices

The unifying function of ch. 1 is supported by short notices which form no intrinsic part of the stories themselves but serve as bonds between them. Thus 2.49 introduces the three friends of Daniel, using their Babylonian names, in preparation for the following story in which these names are employed. It also anticipates the absence of Daniel from that story by placing his friends 'in the province of Babylon' (2.49; cf. 3.1), but Daniel at the royal court. Again, the remark at 5.30 that Darius the Mede succeeded Belshazzar not only rounds off the story by fulfilling the prediction at 5.28 that Belshazzar's kingdom was to be divided and given to the Medes and Persians, but at the same time neatly introduces the following chapter.

The arrangement of the stories

It is possible that the arrangement of the stories in Daniel fulfils a conscious editorial intention. Lenglet has suggested that the Aramaic chs. 2–7 form a concentric structure; 2 being balanced by 7 (four kingdoms), 3 by 6 (persecution and deliverance from death), and 4 by 5, in both of which the king has his future foretold and is subsequently punished. From this observation Lenglet concludes that chs. 2–7 originally formed a unit. This suggestion nevertheless contradicts the chronological framework of chs. 2–6, and ignores the radically different setting reflected by chs. 1–6 on the one hand and ch. 7 on the other (see below); it also prompts one to ask why, if chs. 2–7 existed already as a unit, ch. 1 should ever have been added. In any case, it is not difficult to furnish a plausible account of the arrangement of chs. 1–6: after the setting of the scene (ch. 1) we have the chronological dimension of the four kingdoms set forth (ch. 2); then two 'interpretation' stories are framed by two 'persecution' stories. It may be that the sequence of stories has a structural significance, but the order may do no more than follow that of the monarchs to whom the individual stories had already been assigned.

The four kingdoms

Daniel 2 contains a vision of a statue made of four different kinds of metal which is made to symbolize four successive world-kingdoms. This notion is implied also in ch. 7. A good deal has been written about the existence outside Daniel of a scheme of four world-kingdoms: Babylonian, Greek, Persian and Roman sources have been identified. The Roman source is a fragment attributed to Aemilius Sura, a Roman historian who apparently wrote shortly before 171 BC and presented the empires of the Assyrians, Medes, Persians then Macedonians as leading to the crowning dominion of Rome, over a period of 1,995 years. The same sequence occurs in the fourth Sibylline Oracle (4.49-101). The Sibylline Oracles are a Jewish work emanating from Egypt, but may incorporate non-Jewish material, and the passage in question is thought to be based on a Hellenistic oracle dated to AD 80 but possibly much earlier. Here the reference to Rome's final dominion may be later than the original passage, and there is no eschatological dimension to the scheme: the thrust of the oracle seems to be anti-Greek political ideology, not a philosophy of history. The Persian source presents even greater dating problems, since the texts available are mediaeval. The most important of these, the *Bahman Yasht* tells of a dream of Zoroaster consisting of a tree with branches of gold, silver, steel and mixed iron, representing four periods of time yet to come.

The introduction of metals into the scheme takes us further back to the Greek poet Hesiod (eighth century BC) who, in his *Works and Days* spoke of four (or five) ages of men represented by metals. Each age is successively degenerate—gold, silver, bronze, then iron—the last being the age of Hesiod himself. Many scholars believe that here is the source of Daniel 2 mediated either directly or, more plausibly, through a widespread diffusion of the idea in the Eastern Mediterranean. Finally, G. Hasel has recently suggested another possible source of influence, the 'Dynastic Prophecy' from Babylon, which may be dated to either the Persian or Hellenistic period. It provides a close literary parallel to Daniel's presentation of history, being in the form of a 'prophecy' of successive kings. But the text is very fragmentary, and although four kingdoms may be described in the course of the prophecy, there is no evidence of a four-empires scheme as such.

There is, in fact, no precise parallel to the scheme of Daniel 2; it can be safely said, however, that the idea did not arise independently in Daniel, and that it was used elsewhere in the Hellenistic period as a device of political propaganda against Hellenistic monarchies. Its function in Daniel is not necessarily the same, but the idea of a sequence of kingdoms does play an important part in the construction of the whole book. The arrangement of the stories (and the visions) of Daniel according to a chronology of four kingdoms was quite probably inspired by the dream-statue of ch. 2 itself, and both the vision and ch. 2 may be older than the Hellenistic period. We shall take up the question of the dream-statue and its meaning in the course of the following section.

The history of Chapter 2

We may learn from a study of ch. 2 not only how it was adapted to fit the cycle but also how it had earlier developed into a story about Daniel. In the first place, the present form of the story contains a fundamental contradiction: Daniel is presented *both* as one of the king's wise men (thus presupposing the data supplied in ch. 1) *and* as a Jewish captive unknown to the king. The story runs smoothly until v. 13: the wise men cannot interpret the king's dream and so they are ordered to be killed. According to vv. 13ff., Daniel and his friends are also sought, since they are numbered among the wise. Although (incredibly, in view of ch. 1) not consulted hitherto, Daniel makes an appointment with the king, has the 'mystery' revealed to him, and prays with his friends. But at v. 24 Daniel is shown going to Arioch, the officer in charge of the execution of the wise men, and asking to be brought to the king. Arioch then introduces Daniel as follows: 'I have found among the exiles of Judah a man who can make known to

the king the interpretation'—to which the king replies by asking if
Daniel really is able to offer the interpretation.

Daniel thus meets the king twice: once in the capacity of a wise
man who may consult the king directly, and again in the person of an
unknown Jewish captive who has to be introduced to the king, who
does not know him, by a royal officer. The portrayal of Daniel as one
of the king's wise men is that which coheres with ch. 1, and it is in
fact confined to vv. 13-23. If this block is taken out, we have no
contradiction within the story, but a portrayal of an unknown Jew
who astounds the king, saves the wise men from execution and
achieves a position of eminence at court. This portrait of the hero
obviously conflicts with ch. 1, and it is reasonable to conclude that
vv. 13-23, which are both at odds with the remainder of the chapter,
and also redundant to the narrative, are an insertion designed to
harmonize ch. 2 with ch. 1, and were, most probably, composed by
the author/editor of that ch. 1 (and hence of the entire cycle).

Having identified 'redaction' from 'source' in ch. 2, and found an
earlier form of the story, we can now look more closely at that story
itself. In the first place, it is unusual in that the king, having had a
dream, forgets it and therefore demands to know both the dream and
its interpretation. Is this unique device a means of enhancing the
God-given wisdom of Daniel? Possibly; but the answer may not be
quite so simple, for there is a quite obvious lack of exact correspondence between the dream and the interpretation:

(a)   Elements are present in the interpretation (in vv. 41-43)
      which are absent from the dream, in particular the phrase
      'and the toes' in v. 41a.

(b)   In the dream a stone is cut out 'without hands' and *becomes* a
      mountain; in the interpretation the stone is cut *from* a
      mountain without hands.

(c)   The dream describes a statue of progressively baser materials,
      from gold to clay; the interpretation identifies them as
      successive world-kingdoms which, according to all such
      schemes (including ch. 7) are progressively mightier.

(d)   In the dream the statue is destroyed in a single moment;
      according to the interpretation of the elements of the statue as
      kingdoms, this destruction must have been successive. Indeed,
      v. 44 states that the final kingdom will destroy all the other
      kingdoms.

Points (c) and (d) are perhaps not beyond the kind of variation a storyteller might permit himself. According to Noth, they do not even constitute an inconsistency: a simultaneous destruction of the successive kingdoms is simply a characteristic of Daniel's understanding of history (although ch. 7 does not seem to bear this out). Ginsberg also assumes that a simultaneous destruction of world-kingdoms is envisaged, suggesting that there is an historical explanation: he dates the story to 307-301 BC when 'residual Median and Persian kingdoms' persisted in the form of small principalities. But to explain discrepancy (a), Ginsberg has to propose that the mixing of the iron and clay in vv. 41-43 represents additions to the original story, brought about by the marriage in 252 of the Seleucid Antiochus II and Berenice the daughter of Ptolemy, thus uniting two Hellenistic kingdoms.

Many scholars, including Rowley, have been content to dismiss the discrepancies as of no account, but this is hardly good enough. Rowley's contention that the story is a unified narrative from the time of Antiochus is weakened by the fact that nowehere in it is the presence of Antiochus to be detected, only a fourth kingdom. Quite apart from this observation, however, it is surely important that Daniel interprets the dream successfully—and correctly. Moreover, his interpretation is very important for the overall message of the book. Accordingly, it is reasonable to expect the interpretation and the dream to fit, and when they do not, one is entitled to be puzzled. This is not the sort of occasion when an author is expected to take licences. We must look for a different sort of explanation.

Given that we have evidence that ch. 2 is not a seamless narrative, we are entitled to ask whether the dream and the interpretation do in fact belong to the same piece of cloth, as it were. Is it possible that the interpretation has been patched, like vv. 13-23, onto an earlier story? We cannot be satisfied, however, unless such a suggestion poses a solution to the whole set of discrepancies, for it needs to be not merely a possible, or even a plausible, proposal, but one which solves the difficulties better than any other. Only on such a basis are speculative solutions acceptable.

Let us consider the dream apart from the interpretation. A single statue has a head of gold and feet of clay; it collapses when a miraculous stone breaks it, a stone which then becomes a mountain filling the earth. It is possible, of course, that the dream has no immediate significance for Nebuchadnezzar, but in the two stories of chs. 4 and 5 the message for the king concerns his personal fate. May this statue dream also have concerned Nebuchadnezzar himself? The original meaning of the dream which I have proposed elsewhere is that the statue represents the kingdom of Babylon, of which Nebuchadnezzar is the head of gold and three successors are represented by successively degenerate materials, culminating in either Nabonidus, the absentee ruler or possibly Belshazzar his regent. The statue—the Babylonian kingdom—will fall to a miraculous stone which will become a mountain. The symbolism of the stone is admittedly unclear, but the mountain probably stands for Zion, and the dream depicts the imminent restoration of the Jewish people to their home which will soon become the centre of the earth. (This last suggestion is in any case implied also in the interpretation given in the chapter.) This account of the dream meets all of the difficulties enumerated above. It may reasonably be objected that this is not what the chapter means in its present form. But the importance of the account just given is that it suggests a fairly early date for the original—or earlier—form of this story, probably no later than the early years of Cyrus—whose advent, actual or potential, may have evoked it. It was accordingly refashioned later, in the Hellenistic period, when the interpretation was added to the dream, creating the unique scenario in which the king requires both dream and interpretation, and turning the story into one about four successive kingdoms.

Whether or not we are correct in concluding that the kernel of ch. 2 is a sixth-century tale about an unknown Jew, we have at least been able to catch a glimpse of the kind of history which probably lies behind the story cycle, a history which to some extent disposes of the simple alternative between a sixth-century and a second-century 'date' for Daniel. Rather, the 'date' of the stories covers much if not most of the period in between these two points.

Chapter 5

If ch. 2 perhaps belongs, in its original form, to the sixth century, at the beginning of this long period just referred to, then can we find a story from the other end, in the time of Antiochus? The most plausible candidate is surely ch. 5. Those scholars who have advocated a Maccabean date for the entire book (Rowley is an excellent example) rest a large part of their case on the parallels between Belshazzar in ch. 5 and Antiochus IV. Those who accept the pre-

Maccabean date for the stories have generally ignored these parallels, but there is no reason why this one story should not be as late as this. For ch. 5 is unique among the stories in the important respect that it ends with the destruction of the king. In all the other cases, the king is presented in a better light than here; either he is entirely sympathetic (ch. 6), or neutral (chs. 1 and 2), or finally repentant and even converted (chs. 3 and 4). Note that even in ch. 3 it is 'certain Chaldeans' who initiate the persecution by informing, even though the king becomes 'full of fury' when the heroes reply to his challenge. Indeed, as we shall argue later, the stories appear to be concerned with harmonious resolution of the potential conflict between Gentile and Jewish loyalties. Chapter 5 strikes a note of discord: its message is certainly harsher, introducing the threat of divine destruction to a monarch and the replacement of his kingdom by another.

The message of ch. 5 is thus dissonant with that of the other stories, for while these portray the persecution of Jews because of their refusal to worship other gods, here the Gentile king is depicted in an act of deliberate sacrilege in using Temple vessels for feasting with his concubines and—more significantly—praising 'the gods of gold and silver, bronze, iron, wood, and stone'. Antiochus IV (according to 1 Macc. 1.21ff.—though this may be an exaggeration) also removed the Temple vessels 'with his own hands'.

Another feature of ch. 5 is its reference to earlier stories—the only chapter in which this occurs. Apart from a possible allusion to ch. 2 in the words 'gods of gold and silver, bronze, iron, wood, and stone', we have a formal recapitulation where Daniel is introduced by the queen with the words:

> There is in your kingdom a man in whom is the spirit of the holy gods. In the days of your father light and understanding and wisdom, like the wisdom of the gods, were found in him and King Nebuchadnezzar, your father, made him chief of the magicians, enchanters, Chaldeans, and astrologers (v. 11).

Belshazzar himself also recapitulates Daniel's introduction to the Babylonian court in vv. 13-14, and in vv. 18ff. Daniel rehearses the events of ch. 4. It was this last reference which caused Lenglet to suggest that chs. 4 and 5 were a single story comparing two kings, but another explanation is that the story of ch. 5 is actually a supplement to an existing cycle of Daniel stories, composed in the Maccabean period to reflect its religious crisis, and incorporated into the cycle.

Without the evidence of ch. 5—if we have assessed it correctly—there is no compelling reason to date the editing of the Daniel cycle in chs. 1–6 as late as the time of Antiochus, and almost certainly *a* story cycle was in existence before this time. The remaining stories of the cycle do not give us clues which enable us to posit for them a precise date. However, having established, with the aid of ch. 2 (and perhaps 5) the length of time over which the stories must have emerged and developed, we can attempt to describe their probable background through an investigation of the concerns which these stories display. Our next task, therefore, is to try to understand what sort of people would tell stories of this kind and listen to them. If we cannot find dates for them, we can perhaps at least find the communities among whom, and for whose sake, they came into existence and survived.

The Form and Setting of the Stories

Where, by whom, and for what purpose were the stories of Daniel composed? These really are historical questions, but they can be answered only by considering the forms and themes of the stories themselves, which are literary features. Concentration by scholars on theological/doctrinal and strictly historical problems in Daniel has tended to put into the background an appreciation of the literary qualities of the stories; while the long-standing debate about the sixth-century *versus* second-century dating of the book emphasized either points of historical verisimilitude on the one hand or items of congruity with the Maccabean persecution on the other. The setting and function of the stories, however, can only be understood when they are taken as wholes, and not mined for nuggets of 'evidence' for particular dates or authors.

The stories about Daniel and his friends are not unique in their form. Within the OT itself the Joseph story and the book of Esther share very similar structure and motifs. The apocryphal Daniel stories and 3 Esdras are also very similar, and, outside Jewish literature, the tale of Ahiqar—elements of which have been incorporated into another Jewish 'courtier-tale', Tobit. The most obvious common features are a setting in royal court circles and a hero who rises to eminence in these circles. The hero may be a courtier who triumphs over his rivals or a lowly outsider who proves superior to the king's own wise men. Among other OT stories of this kind,

Joseph is the lowly outsider, Mordecai the courtier; while Moses at the court of Pharaoh (a Hebrew-born member of the royal household) and Esther (an orphan who becomes queen) have elements of both types. In Daniel 2, as we have just seen, the courtier Daniel and the outsider, the 'Jewish captive', are combined, though by means of a process of redaction.

Jewish stories of this genre add a further dimension in the contrast between the supposedly superior culture of the Gentile and the divinely guided, and therefore truly superior, Jewish hero. In the stories of Susanna (attached to Daniel in the Greek version) and Esther this divine providence is at best only implicit; in the Joseph story it is explicit, but not intrusive (see Gen. 39.2; 40.8; 41.16, 25, 39, 51-52), and in the Daniel stories it is prominent. The Jewish hero does not as a rule conquer by his own abilities, but because his God endows him with superior resources. The Jewish hero, then, is not simply an individual hero, but represents his race and his religion, in that it is his own God who provides him with wisdom and opportunity to succeed. While the non-Jewish court tale seems to have been primarily for entertainment, the Jewish court tale, at least as represented in the OT, has a serious, religious aspect. Indeed, two of the stories of Daniel are about physical persecution, which is not a component of the non-Jewish court tale. Two fairly recent studies of the stories by Lee Humphreys and Collins have divided the tales into two categories, Humphreys into 'contest' and 'conflict' tales, Collins into 'tales of deliverance' and 'tales which emphasize the content of the message'. Both scholars distinguish between chs. 3 and 6 on the one hand and chs. 2, 4 and 5 on the other. But ch. 1 can hardly be classified as a 'deliverance tale' (so Collins), though he is right to imply that the content of the message is more definitive of chs. 2 and 5, at any rate, than the element of contest. Putting aside ch. 1, which does not fit either category, and may never have been an independent story, the remaining chapters are best classified as *interpretation* stories (chs. 2, 4 and 5) and *deliverance* stories (chs. 3 and 6).

Each story is different in its own way, but the following elements seem to be basic to the genre:

interpretation story

(a) the king has a vision or dream
(b) the wise men of his court cannot interpret its meaning

(c)   the hero emerges and gives the interpretation
(d)   the hero is rewarded
(e)   the king learns that the hero's god is all-powerful

deliverance story

(a)   the king issues an order which commands Jews to worship an idol
(b)   the hero or heroes are discovered disobeying
(c)   they refuse to comply with the order and are prepared for execution
(d)   they are delivered
(e)   they are rewarded, their enemies punished
(f)   the king learns that the hero's god is all-powerful

As remarked, these stories are a distinctively Jewish form of a courtier tale. The element of jealousy in rival 'courtiers' in the deliverance stories is surely a feature of the basic genre, and it is of course central to the story of Esther. But this feature is present only in Daniel 6, while in all such stories in Daniel the reward of the heroes is of diminished importance. The significant consequence of the deliverance is not the respective fate of the courtiers but the acknowledgment by the king of the demonstration of divine power and hence sovereignty. Indeed, both kinds of story end with the reward of the hero *and* the submission of the king. In this important respect, then, our stories are to be distinguished not only from non-Jewish court tales, but also from the Joseph and Esther stories. They all belong to the same basic genre, but they form a distinctive sub-genre; they all achieve exactly the same climax, and, therefore, emphasize the same 'moral'—the superiority of God's authority to that of the king. Only in the conflict between Moses and Pharaoh do we find plot, and there the plot is not resolved within the genre of the court-contest, but extends into the cycle of plagues and, ultimately, to the crossing of the sea; it provides therefore a very interesting parallel of theme, but only very partly of literary form.

The similarity of the conclusions in all the Daniel stories shows that their collection into a cycle has been governed by the concerns of a coherent ideology. Whether this coherent ideology has been achieved by careful selection, by redaction, or was intrinsic to a particular sub-genre of 'courtier-tale' we cannot investigate here—probably all three alternatives are to an extent operative. But we can certainly ask to what kind of social and religious context the features of these stories, taken as a whole, correspond. Let us consider the character of Daniel and his setting: he is a man of noble blood and Babylonian education who is chosen, and serves successfully, as a royal 'wise man'. The profile is of a man thoroughly Jewish but also thoroughly Babylonian. The wisdom in which he is trained is not the wisdom of the Old Testament as represented in the book of Proverbs, Ecclesiastes, or Job. It is the wisdom of divination; Daniel is one of the company of 'Chaldeans', 'astrologers' and 'magicians', practising a wisdom which believes that the supernatural speaks to men in omens and is concerned with interpreting signs. Daniel may derive his own wisdom from God rather than from his Babylonian education, but nevertheless the kind of wisdom he is given is of precisely the same kind as that claimed by his Babylonian colleagues. Müller has coined the term 'mantic wisdom' for this ethos. What attitude towards the mantic wisdom of the royal court is taken in Daniel? Certainly not a hostile one: the Babylonian wise men are inept, but not denounced. The king is misguided, even to the point of persecuting Jews, but his right to rule is never challenged by the heroes (the peculiarity of ch. 5 was discussed earlier); certain jealous courtiers are condemned in ch. 6 (note their appearance in 3.8 also), but the king is presented as their victim and not as a fellow-conspirator.

The stories, then, all describe a particular setting, the royal court, and a particular ethos, the 'mantic wisdom' of the Babylonians. But it would be wrong to look to the world which the stories describe as the world in which the stories were told. They are stories *about* wise men, but not stories written *by* or *for* wise men. It may seem an obvious distinction to make, but it is one often missed in biblical form-criticism. It is also a very important point of difference between the stories and the visions in Daniel, for the visions, as we shall argue, are probably written *by* men who identify themselves with the kind of 'wise man' Daniel is depicted to be. Müller has argued that the stories originated as *Märchen*, a term difficult to translate accurately: 'folk-tale' or possibly, in this case, 'romance' would be the most appropriate rendering. The power of the 'romance' is its rags-to-riches theme. In this kind of story poor and obscure people rise to riches and fame; orphans become princes, outcasts become kings. According to Müller Daniel began as that kind of hero, but developed into a figure of *Legende*, which as Müller defines it is more ideological, more precisely religious in tone. Here larger interests and

issues clash: religion versus religion, or versus idolatry, the righteous
or moral poor against the wicked and immoral rich, and so on.
Cinderella, on this kind of analysis, is a *Märchen*, the Robin Hood
cycle *Legende*. But folklorist categories are notoriously slippery, and
the precise definitions may be too theoretical for Daniel. Yet what
Müller says does correspond to the observation already made that the
stories are not straightforward examples of a common 'court-tale'
genre, but convey an important religious message, the potential or
actual conflict between Judaism and paganism, between Jew and
Gentile. It is not within court circles that we would expect to trace
this essential component of the stories, but in Jewish communities
living within Gentile society at large. Müller, together with most
critics, recognizes in them *popular* tales, which have arisen from
Jewish communities in the Diaspora, and their theme is, as Lee
Humphreys has put it, 'a life-style for Diaspora'.

How do we know that these stories arose and circulated in the
Diaspora? The answer is that otherwise the stories have no relevance
to the lives of their audience, but function as entertaining anecdotes
about another time and place. The cultural, political and religious
values of these stories simply cannot be set in any other context. We
have already noted, for example, that there is no condemnation of
Gentile rule: on the contrary, the stories extol the aspirations of
pious Jews to high political office. Jews are presented as the king's
most truly loyal subjects (a claim which is made even more explicitly
in the book of Esther). Yet there is also an awareness of the different
'life-style' of Jews and Gentiles. Political acquiescence for Jews is
proper (and no doubt the famous letter in Jeremiah 29 was an
important buttress of this attitude), and cultural assimilation too, up
to a point, for the heroes take (without protest) Babylonian names,
and speak the language of Babylon. But over the Jewish religion itself
there is no compromise. And by 'religion' is meant especially
religious *practice*. In ch. 1 the four heroes reject the king's *diet*
(though the reason for this is not clear); in ch. 3 the heroes disobey a
command to *worship* an image at prescribed times; in ch. 6 it is *prayer*
which is forbidden, and Daniel is found praying towards Jerusalem.
Diet, worship, prayer are thus emphasised as essential—and, of
course, to some extent public—signs of the Jew. No other Jewish
observances are referred to—surprisingly, sabbath, circumcision, and
reading of the law are unmentioned, and there is no hint of
synagogue assembly.

The Diaspora Jew, then, as revealed to us in the stories of Daniel, is defined by his religion and its outward observance, not by language, personal name, or profession. This self-imposed discrimination did not, apparently, provoke any persecution by Nebuchadnezzar or his immediate successors. But we cannot be certain that there never was royal antagonism, nor that persecution did not manifest itself in various forms in lower walks of life. The stories tell us that the Diaspora Jew felt keenly the threat of persecution, and saw himself as defenceless against it. If men of eminence like Daniel could not escape the warrant of execution, could any Jew? There is a good deal of poignancy in the words of the three heroes in 3.17:

> If it be so, our God whom we serve is able to deliver us from the burning fiery furnace; and he will deliver us out of your hand, O king. *But if not . . .*

The Jew cannot be sure of his individual survival in the face of persecution. Whether or not the threat felt was real, whether or not any Jews ever died from persecution, the ambivalence of Jewish life in the Diaspora is eloquently expressed: these stories convey both security and insecurity; political success and martyrdom are equally possible.

The ideology of the Jewish Diaspora which created these stories is not, of course, fully revealed in the stories. We are given a glimpse mainly into the political dimensions. But as we shall see in the next Chapter, the ambiguity of the Jew's political situation is not left unresolved, although it was resolved quite differently in the stories and the visions respectively.

Further Reading

On the figure of Daniel:

J. Day, 'The Daniel of Ugarit and Ezekiel and the hero of the book of Daniel', *VT* 30 (1980), pp. 174-84.

On the genre of the tales:

*W. Lee Humphreys, 'A Life-Style for Diaspora: A Study of the Tales of Esther and Daniel', *JBL* 92 (1973), pp. 211-23.

*Collins, pp. 27-59.

S. Niditch and R. Doran, 'The Success Story of the Wise Courtier: A Formal Approach', *JBL* 96 (1977), pp. 179-97.

H.-P. Müller, 'Märchen, Legende und Enderwartung. Zum Verständnis des Buches Daniel', *VT* 26 (1976), pp. 338-50.

J.G. Gammie, 'On the Intention and Sources of Daniel I–VI', *VT* 31 (1981), pp. 282-92.

On the composition of the cycle:

*P.R. Davies, 'Daniel Chapter 2', *JTS* 27 (1976), pp. 392-401.

P. Lenglet, 'La structure littéraire de Daniel 2–7', *Biblica* 53 (1972), pp. 169-90.

*D.N. Freedman, 'The Prayer of Nabonidus', *BASOR* 145 (1957), pp. 31-32.

*G.F. Hasel, 'The Four World Empires of Daniel 2 Against Its Near Eastern Environment', *JSOT* 12 (1979), pp. 17-30 [gives ample bibliography on this topic].

Other works referred to:

M. Noth, 'The Understanding of History in Old Testament Apocalyptic', in *The Laws in the Pentateuch and Other Essays*, Edinburgh: Oliver and Boyd, 1966, pp. 194-214.

An English translation of the Nabonidus fragment (4QPsDan or 4QPrNab) will be found in G. Vermes, *The Dead Sea Scrolls in English*, Harmondsworth: Penguin, 2nd edn, 1975, p. 229.

On 'mantic wisdom' a convenient description can now be found in J.C. VanderKam, *Enoch and the Growth of an Apocalyptic Tradition*, Washington: Catholic Biblical Association, 1984, pp. 52-59.

5

THE VISION
SERIES

Sequence of the visions

THE HISTORICAL context of the visions does not require as much discussion as that of the stories, for it is generally agreed that they were composed during the persecution of the Jewish community in Palestine by Antiochus IV in the second century BC (ch. 7 being a possible exception; see below). As already remarked, the visions are arranged, and dated, in a chronological sequence which does not continue that of the stories, but parallels it. (The curious note in 11.1, which many scholars take as out of place or secondary, does not seem intended to date the contents of that chapter) But the sequence is not determined merely by the chronological indications; it seems to be intrinsic. For example, ch. 8 refers (v. 1) to the 'vision which appeared to me at the first'; this may be, of course, an editorial link, but other allusions to ch. 7 such as the appearance of the 'little horn', and the 'four winds of heaven', suggest that this vision was quite probably written as a sequel to ch. 7. Again, ch. 9 refers to 'the man Gabriel, whom I had seen in the vision at the first [or: "earlier"]', apparently alluding to 8.16; while the use of 'desolations' and 'desolator' in vv. 26-28 may be inspired by 8.13. The long vision of chs. 10–12 makes reference (11.31) to the 'abomination that makes desolate'—possibly a conflation of the terminology of 8.13 and 9.27. Accordingly, there are grounds for concluding that the visions were *composed in their present sequence*.

Literary unity

Many scholars go beyond this conclusion and assign chs. 8–12 at least, if not 7–12, to a single author. In support of this view is the fact that all four visions (a) reflect the same historical crisis, (b) offer the same sort of explanation for, and resolution of, this crisis, and (c) employ the technique of interpreted revelation to communicate their message. Collins has suggested a more fundamental kinship among the visions: he finds in each of them (d) a different formulation of the same complex of events, whose pattern may be summarized as Past History–Threat–Supernatural Intervention–Salvation, and, in the case of chs. 7, 8 and 10–12, (e) a common reservoir of traditional, and particularly mythological materials.

These similarities, however, do not necessarily mean that the visions were composed by a single author, or that they were composed as a single unit. For instance, the fact that chs. 8, 9, and 10–12 all seem to borrow elements from the preceding visions while sharpening their focus on the climax of history can be interpreted as literary devices within a single composition, but may equally well suggest a process of supplementation, each vision successively building upon an earlier one in order to expand or clarify its message. Such a process, in fact, may well be indicated by 8.26, which reads like a conclusion to an earlier corpus of visions. Similar formulations occur in 12.4 and 12.9. There are also several other indications that the individual visions, and the series as a whole, do have a literary history. The most important of these are the following:

1. Ch. 7 contains some structural peculiarities which betray the existence of two levels of vision and interpretation.
2. The major part of ch. 9 is a prayer which a considerable number of scholars regard as an interpolation.
3. There is an intrusive heading at the beginning of ch. 11.
4. Ch. 12 appears to have been supplemented more than once.

We shall examine these features in turn.

Chapter 7

We have already observed that ch. 7 occupies a pivotal position in the literary structure of Daniel, as a vision composed in Aramaic, and connected thematically and formally with both ch. 2 and chs. 8–12. Several scholars have suggested that, as with ch. 2, what we have is not the original form of the composition. The present text is a mixture of prose and poetical sections (as the RSV shows); this feature itself is hardly a source-critical criterion, although some scholars have made suggestions along these lines. A more useful point of departure is that the ch. as a whole certainly exhibits a curious unevenness. Daniel has a vision of four beasts, culminating in a terrible fourth beast 'different from all the beasts that were before it' (v. 7), and having ten horns. Verse 8 introduces an eleventh horn, and vv. 9-10 introduce a (poetical) description of the heavenly throne, which continues in vv. 13 and 14; but this is interrupted by an account of the fourth beast being slain, while the other beasts only have their dominion taken away: their lives are 'prolonged for a season and a time'. Daniel approaches one of the heavenly beings in his vision and hears the interpretation, a procedure which comes in two parts. First he is told (vv. 17-18) simply that the four beasts are four kings, and that the 'holy ones [often translated "saints"] of the Most High' shall possess the eternal kingdom. But then Daniel asks again, first about the fourth beast, then about the eleventh horn, and here, moreover, his recapitulation of the vision introduces new elements: the fourth beast now has 'claws of bronze' (v. 19), while the horn 'made war with the saints, and prevailed over them' (v. 21), it was judged and its kingdom passed to the 'holy ones of the Most High'. The interpretation which follows speaks of the fourth beast as a terrible kingdom, but concentrates on the horn, and specifically on these features just introduced—its warring against the 'holy ones', and its 'changing times and the law'.

The unevenness may be partly accounted for by the suggestion that the vision originally centred on a fourth kingdom with ten horns, to which an eleventh 'little horn' has been grafted on. This proposal goes back to Sellin and Hölscher early in this century, and has since been advanced, in different guises, by Noth, Dequeker and Ginsberg. There is some linguistic evidence for such a view: the Aramaic in v. 8 *(1)* uses *'ᵃlû* instead of *'ᵃrû* (as elsewhere in the chapter) for 'behold', and employs verbs in the past tense instead of participles. Among stylistic considerations, it has been noted that verse 24 also reads *(2)* awkwardly: 'as for the ten horns, out of this kingdom ten kings shall arise, and another shall arise after them'. Structurally, there is a *(3)* discrepancy between the judgments *on the beasts* in vv. 11-12, where the fourth beast is destroyed and the others spared, and in v. 26 where a court sits in judgment *on the little horn* and removes his dominion. All such considerations can be synthesized into the argument that two different judgment sequences may be read in this vision: one in which a fourth beast is destroyed, comprising vv. 1-14 (vision) and 15-18 (interpretation); and one in which a little horn is

judged, comprising vv. 19-22 (vision) and 23-27 (interpretation). The
two sequences, runs the argument, have been integrated by the
insertion of a reference to the 'little horn' in v. 8, and the grafting ᴏ.
the second vision (of the horn) on to the interpretation of the first
vision.

It is by no means conclusive, but certainly probable, that before
the present rather inelegant vision about an eleventh king of a fourth
kingdom there existed a vision about a fourth kingdom only. Such a
vision was surely composed before the time of Antiochus IV. It has
indeed been argued by several scholars that, in view of its language
(Aramaic), and its closeness to ch. 2, ch. 7 formed an appendix, or
perhaps even a conclusion, to the cycle of Daniel stories, before chs.
8–12 were added. We may reasonably argue that ch. 7 has been
inspired by ch. 2, but this could have taken place before the
formation of the story-cycle. We are hardly in a position to guess
whether this vision was attached to the stories in an earlier form or
not until it reached its present form. It *is* a reasonable guess that in
the time of Antiochus IV there existed a document consisting of chs.
1–7 in more or less their present form—but a guess nonetheless!

The prayer of chapter 9

The bulk of ch. 9 is a prayer (vv. 4-20) which seems out of place in
the visions of Daniel on several counts:

(a) The language and the theology are 'Deuteronomistic': the
troubles of the exiled Israel are explained as due to sin. Nowhere else
in the book is such an explanation of the nation's misfortunes offered;
indeed, such an explanation tends to contradict the implied argument
of the visions that these misfortunes are part of a universal plan, and
intended to test and purify the nation.

(b) The prayer also contradicts the plot of the chapter: Daniel
reads in Jeremiah that seventy years must pass before the 'end of the
desolations of Jerusalem', and prays for an interpretation. This is in
keeping with the tenor of Daniel as a whole; but the prayer becomes
one of repentance, in which God is asked to *act*. In response, Daniel
receives the interpretation of the 'seventy years', for which he had
originally asked, but no divine action.

(c) The juxtaposition of vv. 20 and 21, which involves a clumsy
repetition, looks very much like a seam joining two separate bits of
material.

(d) The prayer itself is in good biblical Hebrew, unlike the remainder of the chapter.

Recently, however, several voices have been raised in favour of the unity of the entire chapter. It is argued regarding (a) and (d) that the prayer may not be from the author of ch. 9, but a traditional prayer which he incorporated; regarding (b) that the explanation of the text of Jeremiah may itself be the divine action for which Daniel prays: God explains why he does not act now, and why he will act soon; and regarding (c) that the repetition in vv. 20 and 21 does not have to be seen as clumsy; or, if it is clumsy, why should the clumsiness not be attributed to the author of the ch. in incorporating the prayer into his composition? The arguments against the original unity of ch. 9 have persuaded more scholars than those in its favour. But there is yet a little more to be said. It has been remarked that without the prayer, ch. 9 is reduced to a very brief scope, a mere ten verses. Could there once have existed such a brief composition? There is no reason why not, and indeed this very brevity, according to many scholars, is the reason why the prayer was added.

But the question still remains: why should this prayer be here, whether original or additional? What purpose does it serve—given that its theology is at variance with the remainder of the book of Daniel? This question has not yet been satisfactorily answered, although with a little research into the *form* of the prayer, a plausible suggestion is at hand. Lacocque has investigated the origin and history of this prayer, and much of what follows here agrees with his results. Other forms of it are found in 1 Kings 8.15-53, Ezra 9.6-15 and Nehemiah 9.6-37. Outside the Old Testament it is also found in a document from Qumran Cave 4 (4QDibHam) and in the first-century AD apocalypse of 2 Baruch. (It also occurs in the Jewish liturgy for the Day of Atonement [Yom Kippur or Yom ha-Kippurim].) The original setting (*Sitz im Leben*) of this penitential hymn is difficult to establish, but there are some themes connecting Daniel 9 with all or some of these instances just mentioned: the time of the evening sacrifice, separation from the Temple, and exile. In Ezra (9.5), the prayer is offered at the time of the evening sacrifice (*Tamid*), as it is in Daniel. In the Qumran text it appears to be the liturgy for the day before Sabbath, but whether or not in the evening is unknown. The prayer of Solomon on behalf of his people in 1 Kings 8 takes place at the dedication of the Temple and declares (vv. 46ff.):

> If they sin against thee . . . so that they are carried away captive to
> the land of their enemy, far off or near . . . if they repent . . . in the
> land of their enemies . . . and pray to thee toward their land . . . *and*
> *the house which I have built for thy name* . . .

Like Daniel 9, this part of the prayer envisages Israel captive in a
foreign land and praying towards their homeland, and specifically
their Temple, which, according to Solomon's prayer, is the place
where intercession is heard. The prayer in Ezra 9 also seems to be
connected with the restoration of the Temple (vv. 8-9). In 2 Baruch
the prayer (like the whole book) is set in the context of the recent
destruction of the Temple (in AD 70). Finally, the exilic setting is
present in 1 Kings 8, in the Qumran fragment 4QDibHam, and quite
clearly implied in Ezra 9.7 and Nehemiah 9.32, 36 (note the phrase
'as at this day').

The conclusions which Lacocque reaches are slightly different. He
regards the prayer as originally composed in Jerusalem during the
Exile. It was, he argues, adopted by the circle responsible for Daniel
because this circle, whom he identifies as a group called *Hasidim*, was
a penitential movement. This ignores the fact that penitence plays
little or no part in Daniel outside this prayer. His suggestion that the
message of ch. 9, including the prayer, is that despite the prohibition
of the evening sacrifice by Antiochus IV, 'nothing and no one is able
to prevent the pious from spiritually being in the Temple and
liturgically offering the daily sacrifices' (p. 142). While this is undoubtedly a part of what the ch. conveys, it does ignore the fact that
within Daniel the ravages of Antiochus are consistently presented
within the framework of the exile of the Jewish people, regardless of
their physical residence in Palestine. For Lacocque, the setting of the
prayer is the liturgy for days of expiation, especially the Day of
Atonement; it seems to us rather more probable that the prayer
stems originally from the liturgy of the exiled community (where it
probably remained even after the so-called 'Restoration'), that it was
directed towards the Temple, and, perhaps, was uttered at the time of
the evening sacrifice, either daily or weekly.

This little study of the prayer does not tell us whether or not it was
incorporated in the original text or added later, but it does show that
it fits with its present context better than its theology leads most
scholars to allow, and that its meaning is not confined to its actual
words, but to the *Sitz im Leben* which its presence invokes.

The intrusive heading of chapter 11

> And as for me, in the first year of Darius the Mede, I stood up to confirm and strengthen him (11.1).

This odd phrase has long exercised the minds of commentators. Who speaks it, and to whom does it refer? What is the purpose of this dating, when the entire vision is assigned (10.1) to the reign of Cyrus? Actually, the entire section from 10.20 to 11.2 is curious. It contains an angelic address with the following structure: the question 'Do you know why I have come?' (10.20a) is answered twice in very similar terms—in order to show, or tell, the truth (10.21; 11.2). Between these essentially two versions of the same answer is an account of the speaker's struggle with the 'princes' of Persia and Greece, with the aid of Michael. (In Jewish literature of this period, the Hebrew *śar* replaces *mal'āk* ['messenger'] as the more usual word for 'angel'. It means a military commander, and implies as a rule a commander of a heavenly army ['host']: 'prince' is a conventional translation.) Then follows the curious statement of 11.1. Many scholars interpret this state of affairs as the outcome of a double version and an explanatory comment, and, following a suggestion by Bevan, Montgomery has proposed an original text of 10.21–11.1 which he translates: ' ... Michael your Prince standing as a helper and as a defence for me'. According to this suggestion, the intrusive reference to the date has resulted in a distortion of the remainder of the passage. But why was the addition supplied in the first place? Taking a quite different line of explanation, one school of thought proposes that ch. 11, with its own dating, should be regarded as a secondary insertion. With this ch. removed, and 12.1 immediately following 10.21 (or 10.21–11.1, reconstructed as above) two links would become visible: Michael's help in 10.21 and his rise in 12.1, and the 'book of truth' in 10.21, referred to as 'the book' in 12.1. The textual difficulty at 11.1 together with the smooth transition created by the removal of ch. 11 make it a plausible suggestion that ch. 11 may be a secondary addition to this final apocalypse, composed or adapted specifically for its present purpose. On this hypothesis, a vision concerned with the prediction of the end-time (chs. 10 + 12) was given added weight by means of a quasi-prophetic account of events leading up to this moment, inserted just before the appearance of the eschatological *dénouement*.

There is no decisive balance of probability, however, in favour either of the original unity of Daniel 10–12 or of the suggestion that ch. 11 is an later intrusion. It is uncertain whether the words 'at that time' in 12.1 require a specific antecedent (which 11.45 provides) or constitute a formal introduction to a description of the eschatological scenario. Compare 'in that day' at Isaiah 24.21; 26.1; 27.1, (6), 12; 28.5; Joel 3.1; Amos 9.11—in these and other cases, the context arguably does provide an antecedent, although some of these passages may have originated independently as eschatological descriptions. But at all events, 11.1 is difficult to see as a part of the original narrative, and its presence surely betrays *some* later modification of the text. Literary critics, who often feel obliged to assume, rather than argue for, the original literary unity of any text, may find it helpful to consider the question of ch. 11 carefully, because Daniel 10–12 is often adopted as a model of the apocalypse form. Without ch. 11, the form is significantly different, with the detailed if somewhat cryptic account of international politics omitted.

The problem of 11.1, then, if intractable, is not without important implications for the composition of what many scholars still regard as the classical example of the apocalypse form. In this connection, the article by Gammie cited at the end of this ch. is interesting, although his attempt to correlate allusions with events in the Ptolemaic kingdom is unconvincing.

The supplementation of chapter 12

Verse 4 of this chapter reads like the conclusion of an apocalypse (see below): 'But you, Daniel, shut up the words, and seal the book, until the time of the end'. However, it is followed by another 'vision-interpretation' sequence in vv. 5-9, where Daniel hears 'a time, two times and half a time', interpreted to him as 1,290 days for the cessation of the daily burnt offering. Verse 9 seems to conclude this sequence with a command to Daniel to 'go your way, Daniel, for the words are shut up and sealed until the time of the end'. Yet the angelic speech continues to v. 13, where for a third time Daniel is given what seems like a concluding command: 'go your way till the end'. A further complication is that v. 12 revises a the calculation of 1,290 days in v. 11 to 1,335. We are hardly confronted with the case of an artist unable to bring a work to a succinct close (Beethoven's symphonies spring to mind), for v. 12 at least is surely a later intrusion which is not even addressed to Daniel, and contradicts a previous datum. The commonly accepted explanation of this verse is that it was added during the period of the Temple's desecration, when calculations of its duration were in need of revision. This attractive and apparently obvious account of the revision, however, runs up against the version of events in 1 Maccabees, which implies that the actual period of desecration was only 1,103 days! It is fitting that a book devoted to the posing and solving of problems should close by presenting a problem to its own interpreters!

We should not forget, amid the evidence of literary complexity, that chs. 7–12 apparently achieved their present form within a space of a few years, probably less. A great deal of literary development might thus seem improbable, although some additions may have taken place after the crisis had passed. Ginsberg has proposed an elaborate literary history in which first ch. 7 was composed as an appendix to the stories (though it circulated separately also) during the reign of Antiochus IV, but before his active persecution; ch. 8 was added shortly after the desecration of the Temple in 167 BC; a third apocalypse, 10.1–12.4 was composed in 165 and then added to chs. 7 and 8, when 8.18-19 was also inserted. Finally, ch. 9 (but without the prayer in vv. 4-20) was composed late in 165, and added to the other three chs., each of which was further altered. The prayer of ch. 9, and 12.11-12, were attached later still.

The literary form of the visions

The recognition of the formal characteristics of ancient literature is important chiefly because form communicates meaning as much as the contents. In reading the visions of Daniel the original audience will have understood them in terms of the literary forms and genres with which it was familiar, and thus have known how to 'take' what it was reading. Equally important, it could recognize the new and different against the typical and expected. In the case of the stories of Daniel it is possible for a modern critic to identify a basic genre and to recognize subsidiary elements and novel features, hoping that the modern perception is not too far from the original. In the case of the visions, the task is very much more difficult. Much of Jewish literature which employs this kind of vision account dates from a later period, some of it perhaps from about the same period, but nothing from an earlier period is close enough to suggest that the readers of Daniel had a clear model before them of what kind of text they were facing. With hindsight, we can classify Daniel with several other ancient texts of the same period and later, but were these texts available to the original readers: did they recognize a distinct 'genre'? If not, the audience will have read the visions of Daniel in the context of those elements in them which were familiar—Old Testament prophecies, dream-interpretations, political pseudo-prophecies known to have existed in Babylon, and, of course, the stories about Daniel, especially ch. 2.

It is common to designate chs. 7–12 as 'apocalypses'. But how useful this term is in furthering our understanding depends on how it is to be defined. 'Apocalyptic' and 'apocalypticism' are notoriously slippery words, and there has hitherto been little agreement about what kind of phenomena they refer to, or how one should set about defining the phenomena. More precision is possible with the term 'apocalypse', for it evidently defines a literary work, and indeed it is applied on the basis of the opening of the book of Revelation: we have therefore a model 'apocalypse' in the New Testament. Nor is there any doubt that Revelation was inspired by Daniel. Recently an attempt has been made by a group of American scholars led by J.J. Collins, to describe a genre 'apocalypse' on the basis of literary forms, contents and religious tenor. To many Daniel, or the latter half of Daniel, is self-evidently an 'apocalypse'. The argument whether Daniel (or part of it) is appropriately defined as 'apocalypse' or 'apocalyptic' is irrelevant here, for it is an argument about what 'apocalyptic' is, not about what Daniel is. However, a discussion of the *usefulness* of the terms 'apocalypse'/'apocalyptic' as applied to Daniel is not out of place.

If we take a reasonably broad definition of an apocalypse as 'an account of a purported revelation of divine secrets through visions or other immediate means' we are able to apply it to all the visions of Daniel. But we should also have to include chs. 2, 4 and 5, which cannot be classified generically with the visions. A more precise, and thus workable, definition of 'apocalypse' might include all or some of the following: (a) a two-stage process of revelation, divided into message and interpretation, and received in a vision; (b) use of symbolism; (b) a concern with explaining the nature of the world and its events in terms of operations in heaven, with a frequent concentration on the eschaton. How do these features apply to the visions of Daniel?

(a) The visionary element in chs. 7–12 comprises sometimes the 'message', sometimes the 'interpretation', sometimes both. Chapters 7 and 8 are similar in having Daniel receive a vision which is later interpreted by an angel; both 7.15 and 8.15 appear to distinguish the 'vision' from the interpretation by the angel. But whereas in ch. 7 there is in effect a single vision, and the angelic interpretation takes place within that vision (v. 16), in ch. 8 the vision ends before the interpretation, which is itself offered in a different kind of vision (v. 18). In ch. 9, by contrast, the 'message' is received not in the form of a vision, but through puzzling over a text of Jeremiah, and only the 'interpretation' is given in a vision—if it *is* a vision. In chs. 10–12 we have again a different set of circumstances: the distinction between 'message' and 'interpretation' does not operate at all.

(b) There is no symbolism in either ch. 9 or chs. 10–12; that is to say, the visions are the appearances of heavenly beings, but not *symbolic* visions.

(c) If Daniel is conerned with revealing the heavenly operations, what is the content of that knowledge? There is very little account given in Daniel of the supernatural world, or of the nature of the eschaton, the 'last things'. It is not even clear whether Daniel has a consistent view in this regard. Is the eschaton understood as the goal of history, with earthly life continuing under the rule of God and his people, or is it some transformation of creation? Only chs. 10–12 seem concerned to address the question of what character the 'end' will have. There is nothing corresponding to the descriptions of the wonderful future age which occur in prophetic poetry like Isaiah 24– 27 (which are also sometimes classified as 'apocalyptic'). Nor do we find any emphasis on the trials and tribulations confronting the righteous immediately before the eschaton; in ch. 11, only vv. 30-35, buried in the middle of the ch., deal with the troubles of the Jewish people; most of the events deal with international relations of little or no relevance to the fortunes of Israel. The content of the revelations in Daniel 7–12 is, if we can generalize, an assertion of *pre-ordained time*: each vision assures that ultimate divine sovereignty is inevitable, but only after those epochs or events which must first fulfil their divinely allotted timespan.

According to the definition of apocalypse we have just been working with, chs. 2, 4 and 5 qualify as apocalypses more readily than chs. 9 or 10–12: they have message and interpretation, symbolic vision, and the content of the revelation is specific—a set of events to

be played out. But we have already classified these chs. as belonging
to the genre of court-tale. It is chs. 7–12 which need classification!
Can we define 'apocalypse' in such a way that all of these chs., and
only these chs., qualify?

This is doubtful. The nature of the problem is, however, that the
relationship between the visions is not best expressed in terms of
literary genre, as is the case of the stories, but in other ways. The
similarities between these chapters are extensive and obvious; the
challenge is to do justice both to these similarities and to the
considerable variety which is equally evident.

The same problem arises in attempting, by using the definition
'apocalyptic', to place Daniel within a well-defined stream of tradition.
Apocalyptic has been regarded variously as the successor of prophecy,
as a recrudescence of myth, and as a spin-off of mantic wisdom. The
fact is that Daniel has drawn from many different streams; if the
search for the origins of 'apocalyptic' forces us to place Daniel
exclusively or even primarily into any one of them, then we are being
hindered rather than helped.

The safest approach to take is that recommended by Porteous,
namely to accept that the visions of Daniel (and hence the book as a
whole) are *sui generis*; this is not to say that they cannot be classified,
only that the readers of the visions at least did not recognize them as
representative of a existing genre, but read them in the light of what
comparable genres they were acquainted with. To approach the
visions from this perspective will not provide an 'objective' reading,
but it will at least not be an arbitrary one. The approach calls for a
description rather than a *definition* of the visions, from which we shall
try to identify some of the more important and obvious influences
upon their creation.

The Danielic visions possess the following features:

1. Although Jewish (and non-Jewish) apocalypses may offer
    revelations about the past, the heavenly geography, or the
    distant future, chs. 7–12 are concerned with an extended
    present which lies between the beginning and the end of the
    sequence of world-kingdoms.
2. However, they successively focus more sharply on the
    immediate present which precedes the climax of history and
    survey, in varying detail, the scope of history from the
    Babylonian exile: chs. 7 and 9 deal with the four world

empires from Babylon onwards; chs. 8 and 10–12 deal with the supplanting of the Persians by the Greeks.

3. The visions teach that the time of the end has been ordained, and that it is near, but they do not discuss what it is like. Only in ch. 12 is there any disclosure about the nature of the end, and even there it is extremely difficult to interpret, and probably deliberately so.

4. In order to present historical knowledge as the object of direct revelation, the visions are given a (fictitious) historical setting.

5. To give the 'revelation' authority, they are ascribed to a reputed wise man.

6. To explain their sudden appearance, they are claimed to have been 'sealed' or 'shut up' until the appropriate time.

7. The revelation of the divine mysteries occurs in two stages; there is, as it were, a text and a translation. The text is usually a vision, but in ch. 9 it is a prophecy of Jeremiah. The text is revealed (or available) to the seer; the translation, or interpretation, is given to the seer, in a vision, by an angel.

Formally speaking, the classification 'vision' is perfectly adequate for Daniel 7–12. There are numerous examples of this literary form in the prophetic literature. In the book of Amos, for example, the prophet sees God holding a plumbline. Unlike the preceding visions, but like the visions of Daniel, this is not an enhanced vision of everyday life—no baskets of fruit, swarms of locusts or fires. The content of the vision is of a heavenly figure, the vision itself is symbolic, its meaning is explained by God after a question-and-answer session with the prophet, and its meaning concerns a divinely decreed 'end'. All or most of these features recur in the Danielic visions. There is a closer resemblance in the visions of Zechariah 1–8, for here the symbolic imagery is more weird (1.18 even mentions four horns), and the interpretation is offered by an angel, not by God. The visions of Zechariah are also about the fulfilment of divine promises; they are not threats of destruction, as in Amos. In such respects, then, the Danielic visions are not essentially different from some of those found in prophetic literature. (For a recent attempt to trace a 'symbolic vision' form from Amos through Zechariah to Daniel, see the work by S. Niditch in the bibliography.) Yet, as we have already observed, not all of the visions in Daniel are symbolic.

Formal classification is complicated by the fact that Daniel 2, which is also a clear influence on the visions, finds its biblical counterpart not in the prophetic vision but in the story of Joseph, which is in no sense of the word a prophetic narrative, but one about wisdom—both the wisdom of practical statesmanship and the wisdom of dream interpretation. The king has a dream, the meaning is unclear till God reveals it through a wise man, the meaning of the dream has to do with the immediate future. We have in Daniel 7–12 a literary *form* which displays diverse origins, but essentially is *a blend of prophetic and 'wisdom' forms attested in the Old Testament*.

The same is true of the *material* of the Danielic visions, but this topic is rather more controversial and has attracted a good deal of discussion, most of which has been framed in terms of the origins of apocalyptic. We shall draw on that discussion insofar as it relates to Daniel. The influences which have been detected on the contents, as opposed to the form, of the visions include the following: i. biblical prophecy; ii. biblical 'wisdom'; iii. so-called 'Akkadian apocalypses'; iv. mythical traditions; v. the tales about Daniel in chs. 1–6; and vi. the historical circumstances of the persecution of Antiochus. While most scholars have wished to insist on some of these to the exclusion of others, it is probable that all of them have made some contribution to what is a rather eclectic literary form.

i. *Biblical Prophecy*

The view that apocalyptic is a 'child of prophecy' has long been dominant, and retains many adherents (see especially Hanson, and, in the case of Daniel, Rowley and Russell). Ideologically, it has been argued, the concern of apocalypses with understanding the divine control of history has been inherited from prophecy, and in particular an interest in eschatology; we have already noted the formal parallels with prophetic visions. As for eschatological conflict, a vision of a final battle between God and an earthly ruler is found in Ezekiel 38–39; where Gog will 'fall upon the mountains of Israel' (39.4); compare Daniel 11.45: ' . . . he shall pitch his palatial tents between the sea and the glorious holy mountain; yet he shall come to his end . . . ' The influence of prophecy has also been argued from the use in ch. 9 of the book of Jeremiah; but this is to confuse prophecy with the *interpretation* of prophecy; interpretation and prophecy are quite different kinds of activity. Daniel certainly contains many allusions to prophetic texts—compare 11.30 with Numbers 24.24 and 12.4 with Amos 8.12, in addition to other references mentioned elsewhere in this book. But this is simply characteristic of a writer who is extremely familiar with his scriptures, whose phrases and ideas come as readily to mind as the writer's own words. Hanson has stressed that both prophets and apocalyptists interpret the events of the real world in terms of the heavenly; both bring messages to Israel from the one to the other. Rowley laid stress rather on the similarity of the mission: the prophets and the writer(s) of Daniel addressed their contemporaries in a time of crisis and revealed God's working in history.

These similarities must, however, be set alongside differences. The prophets appealed to a nation bound in a covenant or quasi-covenant relationship with a national God, whose laws were to be obeyed and who in return had made promises to them. Social and cultic evils brought divine anger, and the prophets warned of the consequences. In Daniel no sins of the people are indicated: what is happening is not punishment, and is no consequence of either the people's behaviour or God's promises to Israel, but is the unfolding of a plan laid down in advance and quite inexorable. The view of history as inaccessible to human influence is radically opposed to what must be seen as typical of Israelite prophecy. Moreover, many of the most characteristic literary forms of prophecy—messenger oracle, salvation oracle, lawsuit, woe—are absent.

ii. *Biblical 'Wisdom'*
The idea that apocalyptic has its roots in wisdom is nowadays chiefly associated with the eloquent argument of von Rad in his *Old Testament Theology*, but the suggestion goes back at least to Hölscher. The main arguments in favour are—as set out by von Rad—the universalist and unitary vision of history, the objectification of the entire historical process, a pessimistic view of human nature in which evil and ultimate destruction are inherent in the world from its creation, encyclopaedic interest, 'charismatic knowledge', and obsession with secrets revealed in code, and with calculation generally. Against von Rad many scholars protested that wisdom shows no interest in eschatology. A plausible reply to this was made by Müller (taken up by von Rad in the fifth [German] edition of his *Old Testament Theology*) that the kind of wisdom reflected in Daniel is 'mantic wisdom', a kind of wisdom familiar in Egypt and Babylon and concerned with divination of the future, astrology and the meanings of dreams. A vigorous argument in favour of associating

Daniel with more traditional Israelite wisdom has been conducted by
Heaton, who closely compares the interests of Daniel and of Ben
Sira. He makes the important point that by the second century BC
the interpretation of prophecy no less than the understanding of
proverbs and knowledge of the world is the prerogative of the scribe.
This comment reduces much of the debate about whether apocalyptic
derives from prophecy or wisdom to sterility: in the Hellenistic
period the two are simply not alternatives. We cannot be confident
that mantic and scribal wisdom were fused together in the schools of
Palestine, although we should note that prudent administration and
mantic proficiency are related in the Joseph story, and possibly in the
career of Daniel also (see 2.48). At the present time, however,
emphasis is being laid on specifically Mesopotamian and mantic
traditions. Another possible stream of influence from this direction
has recently been brought to light by P.A. Porter, namely the *šumma
izbu* series, a collection of tablets from Mesopotamia indicating
anomalous births of humans and animals together with their bearing
on the destinies of individuals and states. Many of the peculiarities
mentioned—multiple heads, eyes in the wrong places, horns of
uneven length—seem to be echoed in the descriptions of the beasts in
Daniel 7 and 8.

iii. *Akkadian Apocalypses*

This term was coined by W.W. Hallo to denote a group of texts from
Babylonia and Assyria; Grayson and Lambert call them 'prophecies'.
According to the latter, these texts are 'descriptions of the reigns of
unnamed kings . . . cast in the form of predictions' (p. 7). According
to Hallo, the sparse information given about the reigns is nonetheless
sufficient to suggest that in many cases rulers of the recent past and
not only of the future are described. Although the texts do not foresee
an end to a linear history, but apparently embrace a cyclical view of
history, Hallo asserts that the linear concept is attested in cuneiform
literature. The closest parallels to these works in Daniel are, obviously,
chs. 8 and 10–12; there are also, however, some related texts 'told in
the first person by a king' (Grayson and Lambert, p. 8), which may
have some influence on ch. 4. As noted in the previous paragraph,
Mesopotamian influence is being increasingly recognized in the book
of Daniel, and although parallels of this kind must always be most
carefully evaulated, the cumulative indications are that foreign, non-
biblical traditions are as significant for understanding the literature

of Daniel 7–12 as they have been shown to be for the court-tales of 1–6. In a recent article, H. Kvanvig has drawn attention to an Akkadian text containing a vision which she suggests as a prototype for Daniel 7.

It is probably under the present heading that we should comment upon a Jewish text from a post-exilic date but maybe earlier than the time of Antiochus IV (more than this cannot be determined) contained in 1 Enoch. Known as the 'Apocalypse of Weeks', it divides the history of the world, from creation until the end, into ten weeks. The course of Israel's history can be traced until the destruction of the Solomonic temple and the dispersion of the nation at the end of the sixth week. Thereafter the nation is apostate, until from the 'eternal plant of righteousness' shall arise a remnant chosen and instructed in wisdom. These are given a sword to execute judgment on the wicked, and 'a house shall be built for the Great King in glory evermore'. After this the angels will carry out a universal judgment, and earth and heaven shall give way to a new creation, in which righteousness shall persist for ever. It is impossible to ascertain whether this text has in any way influenced parts of Daniel 7–12. There are undoubted affinities between Enochic traditions and Daniel, but these affinites extend also to other works such as the book of Jubilees, the Damascus Document and the Testaments of the Twelve Patriarchs; and there are also important differences between 1 Enoch and Daniel which make the question of direct influence difficult to answer. For instance, 1 Enoch and Daniel (and Jubilees) have in common a world-calendar; but while Enoch's (and Jubilees') encompasses the whole period of history, concentrating upon the fortunes of Israel, Daniel's calendar commences (like the Damascus Document) only with the Babylonian kingdom and includes the fate of other nations. Thus, while a number of Jewish works from about the same time as the final composition of Daniel exhibit common interests and influences, they do not provide us with any literary form upon which we can say that the Daniel visions were directly modelled or even directly influenced.

iv. *Mythical Traditions*

Frost, Cross and Hanson, among others, have argued for an intrinsic connection between myth and apocalyptic. In the case of Daniel the rich imagery of the visions, and ch. 7 in particular, has frequently been traced to myth. In the 'great sea' (7.2) is seen the primordial chaotic ocean, Tiamat of the Babylonian Creation Epic, who challenged the sovereignty of the gods, and was defeated by Marduk. In the Old Testament this struggle is between the creator-king Yahweh and the monster Leviathan or Rahab (Job 26.12; Ps. 74.13f.; Is. 51.9-10). The judgment scene in heaven (7.13-14) is now widely thought, following the suggestion of J.A. Emerton, to originate in Canaanite mythology, where the high god El, presiding over the heavenly council, confers kingship on Baal.

Collins has argued strenuously that the visions of Daniel use different mythological materials to convey a certain pattern of events. In each case the 'kingship over heaven and earth is at stake'. Chapter 7, in Collins's view, recapitulates the Canaanite myth of the conflict of Baal over his rival Yamm, and his subsequent enthronement; ch. 8 alludes to the revolt of Helal ben Shachar, the Daystar, to which Isaiah 14.12-15 refers. In chs. 10–12 a mythic system of national deities, or patron angels, appears, in which the 'prince of Israel', Michael, does battle with the 'prince of Persia' and 'prince of Greece' (10.20). In both of these, Collins argues, we also meet the pattern of threat, removal of threat, and state of salvation, so that it is the myth itself, not simply the mythical material, which in each case carries an important part of the meaning. It is actually extremely difficult, in the case of the imagery in Daniel, to decide whether its original context is significant or not. Collins makes an attractive case, but the evidence is by no means as powerful as is required. In ch. 7 the reader is presented with a very brief allusion to the 'great sea' stirred up by the four winds and followed by quite detailed descriptions of four beasts. The four winds, whatever mythical origin they may or may not have, do not belong to the Baal mythology of Canaan; and while it is true that the sea, in Canaanite (and Hebrew) mythology, generates monsters, the monsters described here are not sea-monsters, and their mythological roots, if they have any, lie elsewhere. The evidence points precisely to what Collins denies, a promiscuous borrowing of mythical images. But do these various scraps of imagery form a recognized mythic pattern, namely the conflict of Baal and Yamm? The reading of the Baal text from Ugarit is not a straightforward matter, and it has yet to be proven that the Ugaritic texts *do* describe Baal as being enthroned after defeating Yamm. As for ch. 8, its allusion to the fall of the Daystar is argued from a very small part of the text of ch. 8 and a single allusion to the myth in the Old Testament. Finally the idea of patron deities or angels, while present in ch. 10 (and perhaps also in 12.1) is by no means a prominent element in the vision as a whole. Collins has chosen to make it so, but this interpretation is by no means the only, or even the most plausible, account of what this long vision is communicating.

Of course, in the sense that the visions describe events in the heavenly world, they have much in common with myth. But it remains unproven that Daniel is reproducing any particular mythic plot. As to whether the book itself is mythic, that depends a great deal on how 'myth' is to be defined. Any book dealing with the end of history to be brought about by divine intervention is addressing itself to subject matter appropriate for myth. Indeed, any literature in which earthly events are explained in terms of heavenly activity might be called 'mythical'; but on this definition most of the OT is myth, and, like 'apocalyptic', the term is not especially helpful in understanding the form and function of the visions of Daniel.

v. *The Stories about Daniel*

Several of the features of chs. 7–12 which are also said to be characteristic of apocalyptic are quite obviously derived from, or occasioned by, the fact that the visions are attached to stories about Daniel. Thus, the pseudonymity of the visions, their fictitious ascription to Daniel, is an obvious and inevitable extension of the fictions of chs. 1–6. The weird imagery of the visions, too, is already present (in chs. 2 and 4), as is the sequence of four world-empires which are symbolized. The notion of a 'two-stage' revelation, in which God sends cryptic messages to be decoded by an inspired interpreter, which we have suggested is constitutive of Babylonian 'mantic' wisdom, is carried over into the visions; but since Daniel is now the recipient of the vision, not the purveyor of the interpretation, a new interpreter has to be introduced. It is possible that the interpreting angel is a device borrowed from Old Testament prophetic books such as Ezekiel and Zechariah, but it is unlikely that these texts really provide the *origin* of the device. Presenting Daniel in place of the Gentile king and the angel in the place of Daniel as recipient and interpreter respectively has the effect, of course, of investing the visions with a greater degree of authority, permitting the visions to superimpose their message upon that of the tales. While these features have all been claimed as characteristic of 'apocalyptic', they all have quite logical explanations in Daniel (as Rowley pointed out).

In summing up the literary influence on the visions of Daniel, we can hardly fail to be struck by the variety. When the authors of these visions borrow from myth, prophecy, wisdom or whatever, such borrowings were in many cases made because they were convenient, and not because the authors were 'apocalyptists' bound to a certain tradition. Nearly all attempts to tie down the visions to specific traditions are betrayed by the enormous diversity of sources drawn upon by their authors.

vi. *The Historical Circumstances*

We have not, as yet, looked for the crucible in which these varied materials were fused into a new element. Rowley in particular has insisted that whatever literary and theological heritage Daniel may claim, it owes most to the circumstances that gave it birth—the unprecedented persecution of the Jewish religion by a Gentile king. This period of Jewish history has fortunately bequeathed us a good deal of literature (though perhaps not as much as some scholars think), and we are able to perceive that different explanations of this crisis, and reactions to it, were provoked. The response of Daniel will be explored in succeeding chapters; here we are concerned only with the literary implications of that response. There was a group—or groups—of Jews at this time who found inspiration in the OT books of Joshua, Judges and Deuteronomy, where Israel's right to its promised land was challenged by Gentiles, and where, under the God-given leadership of Moses, Joshua and the judges, Israel won peace from its enemies 'round about', and possessed the land. This ideology emerges clearly in 1 Maccabees, originally written in Hebrew, aiming to reproduce the style of biblical historiography. The crisis itself is attributed to a simple wish by the 'nations round about' to exterminate the Jews, a sentiment which for the author does not seem to have needed any more subtle explanation, although the connivance of 'apostate Jews' is acknowledged. The exploits of the victorious Maccabean priest-kings are at the centre of the narrative. This family had won political independence, Israel had now emerged from centuries of foreign domination, and the new dynasty sought to revive the glorious days of the Davidic empire. 1 Maccabees is, admittedly, written in retrospect, and must be considered as a work of propaganda; but it does show us how in actual fact the historical crisis was met by military and diplomatic resources. 2 Maccabees, on the other hand, while it is also a narrative history, owes more to Greek than Hebrew literary conventions, but its explanation of the crisis is entirely biblical: Israel had brought upon itself these calamities by sin. The answer to Israel's deliverance therefore lies elsewhere than in the military prowess of the Maccabees, for God's anger must be appeased, and this is achieved by the suffering of martyrs. Only when the divine anger is removed is success granted to those fighting for Israel; and the miraculous element in 2 Maccabees remains to demonstrate that the deliverance is more directly a divine than a human work.

Daniel was not, like either of these books, written with the benefit of hindsight. Deliverance lies still in the future. The visions betray no confidence in human valour, nor, apart from the probably secondary prayer in ch. 9, does Israel's sin provide a cause for what is happening. The persecution of Antiochus is rather to be seen in the context of a history of divine administration in which Gentile rulers and their kingdoms are allotted their rôles, a history in which the status of the Jews is one of exile, and in which salvation lies not at all in human effort at either the individual or corporate level. The answer, in brief, is a mystery; it cannot therefore be worked out, but only revealed by God if he so chooses. It is important to bear in mind, however, in the light of all that has been said about the background to the visions, that the single most important cause of the visions is a threat to the Jewish people from a Gentile ruler, a very real prospect of the annihilation of their religion, denial of their sacred history and their God. It was under this pressure that the writers of these visions turned to what was accessible for explicating, in an appropriate literary form, the meaning of the awful prospect. In the literary heritage of the Jewish people—prophetic vision, wisdom, myth—in idioms drawn from the mantic traditions of Mesopotamia, but above all in the stories about Daniel, these writers found a body of literature which provided a suitable combination of theme and literary form: what they saw was Jews dealing with ignorant, idolatrous Gentile kings, heroes miraculously delivered from persecution, but also, perhaps most important of all, heroes who by their wisdom were given to understand—and to proclaim—that God ruled in history, and thus that the Jewish people had a destiny which in God's own time would be fulfilled.

Further Reading

On the composition of the visions:

J.G. Gammie, 'The Classification, Stages of Growth and Changing Intention in the Book of Daniel', *JBL* 95 (1976), pp. 191-204.

H.L. Ginsberg, *Studies in Daniel*.

*Collins, pp. 127-32.

G. Hölscher, 'Die Entstehung des Buches Daniel', *Theologische Studien und Kritiken* 92 (1919), pp. 113-38 [an important and influential analysis, though rather extreme in its conclusions].

(Chapter 7)
M. Noth, 'The Holy Ones of the Most High', in *The Laws in the Pentateuch and Other Essays*, Philadelphia: Fortress Press, 1967, pp. 215-28.

L. Dequeker, 'The "Saints of the Most High" in Qumran and Daniel', *Oudtestamentische Studiën* 18 (1973), pp. 133-62.

(Chapter 9)
B.W. Jones, 'The Prayer in Daniel IX', *VT* 18 (1968), pp. 488-93.

A. Lacocque, 'The Liturgical Prayer in Daniel 9', *Hebrew Union College Annual* 47 (1976), pp. 119-142.

On the definition of apocalyptic:

J.J. Collins (ed.), *Apocalypse: The Morphology of a Genre* (*Semeia* 14), Missoula: Scholars Press, 1979 (ambitious and thorough attempt to define a genre, but does not really work for Daniel).

C. Rowland, *The Open Heaven*, London: SPCK, 1982, pp. 9-72 (a thorough and up-to-date discussion).

(Prophecy)
*P.D. Hanson, 'Apocalypse' and 'Apocalypticism', *IDBS*, pp. 27-34.

*H.H. Rowley, *The Relevance of Apocalyptic*, London: SPCK / New York: Association Press, rev. edn, 1963.

D.S. Russell, *The Method and Message of Jewish Apocalyptic*, London: SCM / Philadelphia: Westminster, 1964.

(Wisdom)

G. von Rad, *Old Testament Theology*, London: SCM / Philadelphia: Westminster, 1962, 1965 (the second edition contains a revision of the section on Daniel and Apocalyptic).

H.-P. Müller, 'Mantische Weisheit und Apokalyptik', *VT Supplements* 22, Leiden, 1971, pp. 268-93.

Paul A. Porter, *Metaphors and Monsters* (Coniectanea Biblica, Old Testament Series, 20), Lund: C.W.K. Gleerup, 1983 (especially pp. 15-29).

(Akkadian apocalypses)

A.K. Grayson and W.G. Lambert, 'Akkadian Prophecies', *JCS* 18 (1964), pp. 7-30.

W.W. Hallo, 'Akkadian Apocalypses', *IEJ* 16 (1966), pp. 231-42.

H.S. Kvanvig, 'An Akkadian Vision as Background for Daniel 7?', *ST* 35 (1981), pp. 85-89.

(Myth)

S.B. Frost, *Old Testament Apocalyptic*, London: Epworth Press, 1952.

F.M. Cross, Jr, 'New Directions in the Study of Apocalyptic', *JTC* 6 (1969), pp. 157-65.

J.A. Emerton, 'The Origin of the Son of Man Imagery', *JTS* 9 (1958), pp. 225-42.

(The tales of Daniel)

*P.R. Davies, 'Eschatology in the Book of Daniel', *JSOT* 17 (1980), pp. 33-53.

Other work referred to:

S. Niditch, *The Symbolic Vision in Biblical Tradition*, Chico: Scholars Press, 1983.

4QDibHam ('The Words of the Heavenly Lights') and the Damascus Document ('Damascus Rule') can be found in Vermes, *DSSE*, pp. 202-205 and 95-117 respectively. 1 Enoch can be found in J.H. Charlesworth (ed.), *The Old Testament Pseudepigrapha. Volume 1: Apocalyptic Literature and Testaments*, Garden City, N.Y.: Doubleday, 1983, pp. 5-107 (with the 'Apocalypse of Weeks' on 74-75), or *APOT*, II, pp. 163-281. Jubilees will be found in the second volume edited by Charlesworth (unpublished in 1984), or in *APOT*, II, pp. 1-82.

6

THE GOD
OF DANIEL

IN DEALING WITH theological, no less than with historical and literary, questions about Daniel, we must pay attention to its two voices. Half of the book was originally addressed to Jews who were exiled, but living actually or potentially fruitful lives in Gentile domains, lives in which questions of divided loyalty arose, but for whom nothing beyond the *status quo* was of immediate concern. The other half of the book was written for a nation for whom the Gentile world had broken destructively into its own life and land, for whom persecution was an urgent reality, not a mere threat or even an occasional pestilence, whose future as the people of God was in question, and for whom no ready explanation lay to hand. Not least of the problems was the division which the persecution deepened within the Jewish community on such questions as the nature of true loyalty, of the covenant, of the power and will of the Jewish God.

These two different voices with their contrasting 'theologies' must be heard both distinctly from each other and also in harmony. The juxtaposition of the two parts of Daniel creates a tension within the book which is theologically fruitful; indeed the tension itself may reflect the uncertainty and division of opinion which the crisis under Antiochus IV brought about in the Jewish community. It would be wrong to insist that the visions have the last word. In underlining the tensions in the book, the modern interpreter, reacting critically and in a different historical and theological climate, is responding positively, not negatively, to the critical issues with which the book of Daniel grapples.

The nature of God

The names by which God is referred to
Forms of reference to God provide a concrete and instructive
illustration of Daniel's perception of the deity. They fall into three
categories:

(a) Terms familiar from elsewhere in the OT: in the prayer of ch.
9, which did not originate as part of the book, and reflects Deuterono-
mic idiom, we find the divine name Yahweh, but also its alternative
'adonay ('the Lord'), which by the second century BC may already
have been the accepted way of pronouncing the divine name; it is also
found at 1.2. Elsewhere in ch. 1, and in the (secondary) prayer of
2.20-23, we find 'God' and 'God of my fathers'.

(b) Other titles for God: 'God of heaven' is the most common term
in ch. 2, where Nebuchadnezzar also acknowledges him as 'God of
gods and Lord of kings'; 'God of Gods' recurs in 11.36. In chs. 4 and 7
the usual appellation is 'Most High'; in ch. 5 'Most High God' (as in
3.26).

(c) With a possessive: In the persecution stories this is common: in
ch. 3 the three heroes speak of 'our God' and others of 'their own
God' and 'the God of Shadrach, Meshach and Abednego'. In ch. 6 we
find 'my God' and 'God of Daniel'.

To oversimplify somewhat, we find (a) 'lord' in Jewish prayer, (b)
honorific, universalistic titles in public contexts, and (c) the emphasis
on the personal in instances of persecution. Since we have taken the
prayers in Daniel 2 and 9 to be secondary, let us concentrate on the
last two categories.

'Most High (God)' is a term apparently acceptable to both Jews
and Gentiles. It occurs in the OT as a designation of the God of
Israel, but in contexts involving foreigners, for instance Balaam
(Num. 24.16), Melchizedek (Gen. 14.18) and the king of Assyria (Isa.
14.14). In Mark 5.7 and Acts 16.17 it is also used of God by,
respectively, the Gerasene demon and a possessed girl, and was in
widespread use in the syncretistic Hellenistic-Oriental world. The
title was also used on coins of the Hasmonean kings. 'Most High
(God)' is thus a designation for the God of Israel which was
acceptable to both Jews and Gentiles. It is a term of compromise and
not of confrontation, and we find it mainly in stories in which the
God of the Jews is co-operating with the Gentile monarch, by
presenting him with symbolic revelations subsequently to be

deciphered. However, in cases where God is acting against the monarch, in defending Jews against persecution, he is 'their God'. The designations of God, therefore, are not carelessly expressed, but chosen to reinforce the ambiguous relationship between God, Jews and Gentile king.

God and other deities

It is often stated in commentaries that paganism is a major target of our book. But while the heroes bear Babylonian names probably compounded with Bel, Nebo and Marduk (their derivation is not always certain, for they are a little garbled), these gods themselves play no part in the action. Many commentators have stressed the importance of the theme of idolatry in Daniel, and especially in ch. 2 (see especially von der Osten-Sacken). But it is doubtful whether idolatry is here an issue at all. The incompetence of the Babylonian wise men in ch. 2 is said to be a symptom, not of the impotence of their gods, but of their inaccessibility to the wise men (v. 11):

> The thing that the king asks is difficult, and none can show it to the king except the gods, whose dwelling is not with flesh.

There is no contest between the Jewish God and Babylonian gods here, except by the faintest of implications. The king, finally, acknowledges (v. 47):

> Truly, your God is God of gods and Lord of kings and a revealer of mysteries, for you have been able to reveal this mystery.

The king is impressed, but not converted. Indeed, he offers incense and homage to be offered up to Daniel! There may in this be a faint element of mockery on the part of the story-teller, but we cannot be sure. In ch. 3, however, idolatry is indeed an issue, and there are direct references to Babylonian gods, although they are not named. Instead we have rather vague statements: in v. 12 the king's officials report that the Jewish heroes 'do not serve your gods or worship the golden image which you have set up' (recapitulated in v. 14), and in vv. 28 and 29 the king acknowledges that the heroes would not worship any other god, nor was 'any other god able to deliver in this way'. Indeed, it is fairly obvious that the real issue, as stated at the outset, is the worshipping, not of Babylonian gods, but of an 'image of gold'. Every time the image is mentioned, it is referred to as 'the image which King Nebuchadnezzar has set up' or 'which you have set up', the implication being, perhaps, that the image is in effect an image of Nebuchadnezzar's majesty. If it is the image of a Babylonian god, we are not told as much. Indeed, the conflict is fundamentally *not* about the worship of other gods. The crime of the Jews is to disobey the king, who is setting himself up against God: 'Who is the god that will deliver you out of *my hands?*' (v. 15). The outcome of this story is a prohibition against speaking anything against the God of the heroes, for the king will punish them severely. Instead of being a rival god himself—which is how he began—the king becomes a protector of their god from blasphemy!

Chapter 6 more straightforwardly describes the same situation: the plot is set in motion by the thesis that only the king may receive petition. The outcome is that those who hatched the plot are victims of their own conspiracy, and all the king's subjects are to 'tremble and fear before the God of Daniel'. There are no pagan gods here, and we find, not theological polemics against idols, as is the case in Second Isaiah, but the political problem of the Jews' insistence on worshipping their own God in their own way. The Jew is victimized *as a disobedient subject of the king*, not as one who impiously rejects the local deities. The Jews' God, and his power, are being opposed not to other gods, but to political powers, be they kings or courtiers. Indeed, the problem of all the stories is not whether Judaism is *theologically* acceptable to Gentile rulers, but whether it is *politically* acceptable. This issue, of course, arose in different ways in the Jewish Diaspora and under Antiochus IV, and the stories and visions of Daniel offer different resolutions, which we shall consider in due course. But the issue is the same throughout the book: it is the divine claims of kings which have caused the conflict with Jewish religion, not the claims of other deities.

The God of Israel

As we have just seen, in the stories God is represented as showing to the king that:

> ... there is a God in heaven who reveals mysteries, and he has made known to King Nebuchadnezzar what will be in the latter days ... (2.28).

God also reveals, for the benefit of the king, the interpretation:

> not because of any wisdom that I have more than all the living has this mystery been revealed to me, but in order that the interpret-

ation may be made known to the king, and that you may know the
thoughts of your mind . . .

In ch. 2, the result is that the king acknowledges the greatness of this
God (vv. 46ff.). But in ch. 4, God is teaching the king a lesson; the
result here is that Nebuchadnezzar

> blessed the Most High, and praised and honoured him who lives
> for ever . . . Now I, Nebuchadnezzar, praise and extol and honour
> the King of heaven; for all his works are right and his ways are
> just . . .

Praise, honour, and of course, repentance (ch. 4) are accepted from
Gentile kings, but not their conversion. They are to respect the rule
of the Jewish God, but they are not required, or expected, to become
Jewish. The latter is a solution to the problems of the Jewish
Diaspora which Daniel rejects. The Judaism of our book is not
proselytizing. One feels that in the Diaspora such a solution would
have been not only unrealistic, but also unacceptable. There would
never be a universal embrace of Judaism; conversely, there would
always be a Jewish people. There is, correspondingly, some emphasis
on the distinctiveness of Jewish religious practices: ch. 1 makes much
of Jewish belief in the significance of diet and ch. 6 of the duty of
regular prayer, not to mention the refusal to bow down to images in
ch. 3.

In the visions, the Jewish-Gentile relationship has undergone a
drastic transformation. There is an emphasis on the Jewish people as
a *nation*. In ch. 7 they are the 'holy ones of the Most High' who will
succeed all other earthly kingdoms; in chs. 10–12 we find constant
reference to the 'people' (10.14; 11.14, 32, 33; 12.1 [twice]) and to the
prince who 'stands for them', Michael (10.13, 21; 12.1). The marks of
personal piety which characterize the model Diaspora Jew in the
stories, where they are mentioned at all, have a different significance:
in 10.3 Daniel's mourning and fasting, far from being part of regular
and public Jewish observance, seem to be peculiar preparations for
the reception of a vision. The exemplary Jew of the stories is replaced
in the visions by the suffering, but soon to be vindicated, nation.
Correspondingly, the Gentile kings and kingdoms are destined for
destruction. In ch. 2 we are given a picture of successively degenerate
kingdoms; in ch. 7 they are successively more brutal, and instead of
the Gentile king who needs enlightenment and correction, as in the
stories, we are shown a procession of beasts whose destiny is

perdition. In a nutshell, the stories are about harmony between Jew
and Gentile, overseen by a providential God, the visions about a
definitive confrontation between Gentile and Jew, or, more accurately,
Gentile king and God. Here God is the final destroyer of all Gentile
kingdoms, and the only immediate resolution to the present crisis is
the advent of a Jewish kingdom. This is a quite different solution
from that of the stories—but quite different circumstances provoked
it. There is also, of course, a continuity between stories and visions:
the issue is not one of a clash of religions, but of politics—not whom
one should worship, but who rules history. The challenge to God
comes not from other gods, but from human kings.

The God of history

Under this single heading we may consider three intrinsically related
characteristics of God which are emphasized in Daniel. God *knows*
all, he *controls* all, and he *rescues*:

> He changes times and seasons; he removes kings and sets up kings;
> he gives wisdom to the wise and knowledge to those who have
> understanding . . . (2.21).

> He delivers and rescues, he works signs and wonders in heaven and
> on earth (6.27).

In ch. 2, what is at issue is clearly the omniscience of God. It is not
simply that God has given Nebuchadnezzar his dream, nor that he
has also provided the interpretation. It is more: what has been
revealed is the future, and only the God who controls the future can
reveal it. The God who has revealed the dream is the same God who
will fulfil it (v. 44). What the interpretation claims is that the
succession of kingdoms is in the control of this God, and the
interpretation is a demonstration not so much of the mantic power
derived from God, but of his control over history. This control is
illustrated in a more concrete manner in ch. 4, where again
Nebuchadnezzar is given a dream. The purpose of this dream is
made quite explicit:

> The sentence is by the decree of the watchers, the decision by the
> word of the holy ones, to the end that the living may know that the
> Most High rules in the kingdom of men, and gives it to whom he
> will, and sets over it the lowliest of men (v. 17; cf. v. 32).

It may be that some act of hubris on the part of the king has provoked

God to humble the king, but no such act is mentioned. We read only that the king's greatness

> has grown and reaches to heaven, and your dominion to the ends of the earth (v. 22).

Interestingly, however, it is suggested that if the king were to 'break off his sins by practising righteousness' and his 'iniquities by showing mercy towards the oppressed' (v. 27), there might be a 'lengthening' of his 'tranquility'. As remarked earlier, the requirements laid upon a Gentile king fall short of the demands of Judaism: adherence to acceptable moral standards is all that is expected. But even so, these words are not a call to repentance in order to avert the fate predicted, for what has been foreseen has been decreed. Yet we may note in this verse something less than a total and rigid determinism. One cannot avert the inevitable, but one may postpone it. Contrast the case of Hezekiah in Isaiah 38.1ff.: because of the king's prayer, he will not die as God had told him, but will have fifteen years added to his life. As a sign of this grace, the sundial moves backwards. Time goes into reverse. Here, however, there is no turning the clock back, for history has its own inexorable course to take. (Another interesting comparison may be drawn between the response to divine punishment by Nebuchadnezzar in Dan. 4 and the irresponsible comment of Hezekiah in Isa. 39.8.)

In the visions, the sequence of world events is at a greater remove from the time of Daniel than in the stories, and in chs. 10–12 the detail is such as to imply that the course of history has been ordained to the minutest degree. This is doubtless an assurance to those suffering persecution. Even their own misery has been foreseen, yet its end will not be delayed, for it can be measured in days. Here we find another contrast between the stories and the visions. There is little or no place for divine intervention in history in the visions. The historical process unfolds as planned, and the God behind it all becomes visible only at the last. Providence consists in God's foreknowledge from the beginning and his final intervention, but between these two extremes of history there is no room for divine action. In the stories, as we have seen, although we find that God is the God who controls because he knows, there nevertheless remains a place for the miraculous rescue. In the tales the ultimate end of history is of no pressing concern. If the visions look for God at the end of history—because they do not find him in the present?—the stories look for God in the everyday.

There are two stories of miraculous deliverance, each of which culminates in a royal confession:

> There is no other god who is able to deliver in this way . . .

> His dominion shall be to the end. He delivers and rescues, he works signs and wonders in heaven and on earth . . . (3.29; 6.26f.).

Thus, in the stories the Jew looks for his God to rescue him 'on earth', in the here and now (although he is never so arrogant as to expect it—see 3.18). In the visions, the Jew does not look for any such intervention in the ongoing process of history; and because he does not, he expects it at the end. But in this important contrast there is again a continuity: the belief remains that God *will* deliver, because he is the God of the Jews, he is just, and he is the lord of history.

Further Reading

On anti-idolatry in Daniel:

P. von der Osten-Sacken, *Die Apokalyptik in ihrem Verhältnis zu Prophetie und Weisheit* (Theologische Existenz Heute, 157), Munich: Kaiser, 1969.

On divine control of history:

D.S. Russell, *Method and Message of Apocalyptic*, London: SCM, 1964, pp. 205-34 (chiefly 230-34).

On the salvation of Israel and judgment on Gentiles:

Russell, *Method and Message*, pp. 297-303.

7

THE JEWISH HERO
AND
THE GENTLE KING

HAVING LOOKED AT the nature of God in the previous chapter, we ought now to consider the human protagonists. There are four classes of humanity in the book of Daniel: the wise Jewish hero, the Gentile monarch, the Jewish nation, and 'those who are wise' (who appear as a distinct group only in ch. 12). In this chapter we shall deal with the first two; the succeeding chapters will consider the last two.

The Jewish hero

Although heroes of legends or folklore are rarely representative of those who tell and hear of them, it is probable that the ordinary Diaspora Jew would have in some measure identified himself with Daniel and his friends. Certainly, the ordinary Jew did not attain high office, nor undergo their trials; but in the telling of the stories, one may infer, the Jew in the Diaspora found an outlet for expressing his own hopes, doubts and fears. Thus, the heroes to a large degree serve as models for all their fellow exiles, and in the stories we may look for some expression of the theology of Diaspora Judaism, especially concerning its attitude towards God and towards Gentiles.

In ch. 1, the heroes are taken into the royal court to learn the 'letters and language of the Chaldeans', an education which occupies them for three years. They also accept Babylonian names. But the 'rich food which the king ate' and the 'wine which he drank' are refused, on the grounds that these would defile. There is a problem here which many commentaries do not face. Jewish scruples against eating or drinking with Gentiles can be documented from the Hellenistic period (e.g. Jubilees 22.16), but this is not what the heroes refuse: they accept the vegetables. Many scholars take the view that the heroes are conforming strictly to Jewish dietary laws in their refusal, as the use of the verb 'defile' suggests. But no Jewish dietary laws require vegetarian intake only, and wine is forbidden only to Nazirites. It is possible—as is generally surmised—that the story in its present form has been influenced by the Maccabean crisis in which many Jews, we are told, were forced to eat unclean foods. Yet the heroes' diet is not made explicitly a issue of law or even of religion. They do not eat 'Jewish' food, nor insist that the food be prepared by Jews according to certain requirements. The story does not, therefore, imply that Jews may not eat Babylonian meat or drink Babylonian wine, just as it expresses no alarm at the taking of Babylonian names, service in the Babylonian court, or the acquisition of a Babylonian education. What, then—if any—is the point of this demonstration?

Let us first note that, in the light of the heroes' adoption into the court and the Babylonian way of life, this stand over food seems somewhat inconsistent. As a gesture it makes sense only if it is intended to underline, at the outset of a career at court, that there is a limit to the allegiance of these Jews to Babylonian values. Our heroes make the point that fine food and drink are not what sustain life, but God. Indeed, this message is conveyed quite explicitly in the statements that it was God who enabled Daniel to approach the chief eunuch (v. 9), and, more significantly, 'gave [the youths] learning and skill in all letters and wisdom' (v. 17). Such remarks do not contradict the impression that the heroes derived wisdom from their education at the court, but merely establish the ultimate origin of that wisdom. In this chapter, then, the issue is not of values—food, learning, language, names—but the *origin of value*. The issue of food and drink is a symbolic, not a concrete, issue. It is not a matter of the right of Jews to conform to a peculiar regimen, but is, in fact, a demonstration. What exactly is demonstrated? Not that a diet of vegetables and water is better for your health, nor that the Jewish physique is improved by deprivation! These Jews are guests of the king, from whom they accept everything—names, education, and food. The extent of their allegiance to Babylonian culture must not be gainsaid: the whole chapter strongly affirms the propriety of such cultural assimilation. But does this assimilation not imply that the king is their provider? The dietary experiment proves that the king is not. The point made is not a cheap one. This opening chapter draws for the reader that boundary which circumscribes the allegiance of the Diaspora Jew to his monarch. In the stories to follow, that boundary is reached time and again: the Jew may conform entirely to every item of the king's will, but not to the point of acknowledging the king's absolute sovereignty. This first Daniel story, like the stories of chs. 3 and 6, defines both positively and negatively the character of Jewish political allegiance.

Throughout the stories, the antagonism between Jew and king is muted where it is not absent, and it pertains legitimately to one issue only: that of ultimate sovereignty over Jewish lives. Chapter 2 expresses most clearly a concern for the welfare of Gentiles, a concern which is far more prominent in the stories:

> Therefore Daniel went in to Arioch, whom the king had appointed to destroy the wise men of Babylon; he went and said thus to him, 'Do not destroy the wise men of Babylon; bring me in before the king . . . , (v. 24).

Daniel's intervention is, in the first instance, in order to save the wise men (compare v. 18 which is secondary and where the motivation is self-preservation; but this is dictated by considerations of plot as much as of ideology). Concern for the king is also to the fore: God has revealed to him what will be; he is troubled; Daniel seeks to reveal to the king the 'thoughts of his mind'.

The king's relief, in turn, motivates his reward to Daniel. So far as human intercourse is concerned, we learn from this story that Diaspora Judaism is not to be a self-regarding and enclosed society, unmindful and uncaring of its Gentile neighbours. We can see why: the themes of concern for all citizens and of political advancement go hand in hand. This story says, in effect, that no subject is more altruistic than the Jew, and consequently, no subject is more worthy of advancement than the Jew. The openness of Diaspora Judaism to its social and political environment, as illustrated in this and other stories, is remarkable. The theological grounds for this openness, furnished in ch. 4, will be explored presently when we consider the Gentile monarch.

The refusal of the king's food in ch. 1 was, we argued, a symbolic denial of the king's implicit claim to be sole provider. Similarly, the claim of the king to religious authority over all his subjects is rejected by the heroes in chs. 3 and 6. We shall use ch. 3 as illustration. The king's edict implies the right to enforce religious worship, and supports that claim, significantly, with the threat of death. This is

precisely the converse of the claim to provide life which, we have
suggested, is implicit in ch. 1. The story is about the sovereignty of
life, for the contest is not between rival gods (as we showed in the
previous chapter), but between God and the king. Which has the
power over life? The story gives a more complicated answer than its
mere outline suggests. Certainly, with all the dramatic trappings of
the extra heat and the fate of the stokers, the story builds into a
magnificent contest. But there are two highly important marks, the
first in v. 18 and the second in v. 25. While the story inevitably
proclaims triumph, v. 18 actually expresses the perspective not of the
author but of the intended victim: no matter what the outcome, the
heroes will not obey the king's command. In v. 25 an apparently
superfluous detail arises as the king exclaims in astonishment:

> But·I see four men loose, walking in the midst of the fire, and they
> are not hurt; and the appearance of the fourth is like a son of the
> gods.

These two verses point beyond the superficial reality of miraculous
deliverance. Why? Because, perhaps, these persecution stories do not
simply create imaginary confrontations to delight the Jew with
vicarious triumph over his Gentile masters; they address a legitimate
fear. Persecution, whether or not mortal, is perhaps an ever-present
anxiety. Such an anxiety cannot be met adequately by miracle
stories. The fiery furnace is not escaped in real life with the aid of a
deus ex machina. What if relief does not come? The fact is that the
winning of a fire-contest may convince the king of God's power, but,
conversely, *no lack of divine intervention will convince the Jew of
God's impotence*. Diaspora Jewry, as it speaks through this story,
does not require miracles to vindicate its faith in the saving power of
its God. But it has, perhaps, a right to a token of divine presence. The
fourth figure in the flames is a mysterious entity, having the form of a
'son of the gods'. It is surely idle to guess the name of this heavenly
figure, since the narrator obviously does not intend us to know. It is
evidently not his identity but his function which matters, whoever he
is. He symbolizes the Jew's conviction that in the fire, whether or not
he will escape, he is not without God, and thus not without
vindication.

The profile of the Jewish hero in the Daniel stories embraces the
extremes of possibility: exalted political prince and persecuted victim.
Each rôle reflects a different face of the Gentile monarch; together

they define the limits of Jewish participation in the life of its place of exile.

The Gentile monarch

The Gentiles as a group are not represented in the book of Daniel, either in story or vision (contrast the 'nations' in Deuteronomy, the Second Isaiah or Psalms). Rather, Daniel presents us with four profiles of the Gentile king, described, from most to least favourable, in chs. 6, 4, 3 and 5 respectively.

In ch. 6 occurs the most generous portrayal of the Gentile monarch. The description of a rather dull-witted but benign Darius tallies with that of Ahasuerus (Xerxes) in Esther; both kings are the dupes of jealous courtiers. The goodwill of the king towards Daniel is clear from v. 3, where he intends to 'set him over the whole kingdom'. This provokes a conspiracy among other courtiers, who entice Darius into issuing a seemingly innocent edict by which Daniel may be ensnared. Learning of the outcome, the king is distressed, 'and set his mind to deliver Daniel; and he laboured till the sun went down to rescue him'. When it transpires that the 'law of the Medes and Persians cannot be changed' (again, compare Est. 1.19; 8.8), it is Darius himself who calls out, 'May your God, whom you serve continually, deliver you!', then spends the night fasting and sleepless. At Daniel's deliverance he is 'exceeding glad' and finally decrees that 'men tremble and fear before the God of Daniel, for he is the living God, enduring for ever . . . '

In this story, then, the divine deliverance relieves the king hardly less than the Jew. Both are allied against treacherous courtiers. For the Diaspora Jewish audience, the story promotes the monarch as their ally and defender, while stressing that in this rôle he is by no means omnipotent, for only God can in the end secure his people's well-being. But we may guess that the story was aimed also at Gentiles, reassuring them that the interests of the Jewish people were fundamentally those of the king, since even when Daniel explicitly disobeyed the royal command, that command was seen to be against the intention of the king. The story also warned those who would provoke antagonism between king and Jew that the fate they plotted for others would become their own. Of the greatest *theological* importance here, however, is the identity of interest between the king, God and God's people. There *is* no real conflict of interest between human and divine sovereignty, and perfect harmony under the supreme authority of God is both possible and to the benefit of all.

Such a conflict may nonetheless be generated, and in ch. 4 it is, unusually, resolved without any danger to the Jewish subject. On the contrary, it is the Jew who brings about the necessary reconciliation. From whence is the conflict generated? Verse 27 hints at a lack of justice on the king's part, but this failing is not to be given any great significance. It is unmistakably the king's own splendour which constitutes the problem and provokes the divine reaction. The king has committed no sin for which punishment is due, but he has fallen into a condition in which he needs a lesson. The king is not being chastised for his sins, but reminded of the relativity of his status. In the vision, the tree becomes strong 'so that its top reached to heaven, and it was visible to the end of the whole earth' (v. 20). The height of the tree suggests hubris (there is a possible allusion to the tower of Babel, Gen. 11), and the king's pride is manifest in v. 30:

> Is this not great Babylon, which I have built by my mighty power . . . for the glory of my majesty?

As the king speaks, the vision is fulfilled, and the king is humbled. Finally he is not only restored, but 'still more greatness' is added to him, while he confesses that God is able to abase the proud. (Incidentally, the confession that none can say to God, 'What doest thou?' [v. 35], and the manner of the restoration are reminiscent of the story of Job.)

Human kingship, this story teaches, is a gift of God. He gives it, he takes it away; he requires from the king only acknowledgment of his ultimate sovereignty. The message is stated succinctly in v. 32: 'the Most High rules the kingdom of men and gives it to whom he will.' There is, then, some conflict between the Gentile king and God. But it takes place, as it were, within the king's own heart and mind, and is resolved by the acknowledgment on the part of the king that his own sovereignty is derived, not absolute.

Chapter 3 teaches the reader—and the king—the same lesson, but in a different mode. The issue is indeed sovereignty, but this sovereignty is settled by a kind of 'trial of strength'. The challenge is between the power of Nebuchadnezzar and of God over the life and death of the three heroes. The king acknowledges defeat appropriately:

> Blessed be the God of Shadrach, Meshach and Abednego, who has ... delivered his servants, who trusted in him, *and set at naught the king's command.*

The king is depicted here unsympathetically; although he acknowledges defeat and exalts the three Jews, there is a certain edge to this story not present in either ch. 6 or 3. In contrast with ch. 6, the king is now identified as a potential persecutor of Jews, whose grudging acknowledgment of defeat offers a less reassuring resolution than the joyous relief of Darius. This contrast may point to different experiences under Gentile rule, but not necessarily: it really reflects *different perceptions of the same problem.* That problem is the fact of Gentile rule, its acceptability to God, and its implication for Jews. Is it benign, or is it (potentially, at least) malign?

We might expect a third option to appear: a rejection of Gentile rule as symbolized by an evil ruler. But the evil ruler Belshazzar, in ch. 5, is no persecutor of Jews. For the central problem of Gentile kingship in these stories is never the attitude of the king to Jews, but his attitude (or lack of it!) to the Jewish God. We do not find any 'anti-Semitism' in these stories, and no one is persecuted simply for being Jewish. The conflict always develops over a concrete issue, and one in which the absolute sovereignty of the king is denied by the Jew. The ultimate story of ultimate confrontation—ultimate in its consequences—is one of sacrilege, not genocide, of direct challenge to God, not indirect. Belshazzar takes Temple vessels, issues them to his nobles, wives and concubines, and drinks from them while praising 'the gods of gold and silver, bronze, iron, wood and stone'. It is tempting to see in these materials an allusion to the statue of ch. 2 and thus symbols of human empire. If this interpretation is followed, the idolatry is towards human kingship. At any rate, as we have commented earlier, the gods referred to are not named, and it is not they who do battle with the Jewish God, but their champion Belshazzar. The terms of the challenge are such that it can only be met, as it is met, by the destruction of the king. His rewarding of Daniel for predicting disaster is not as incongruous as it seems, for it is significantly different from other chapters. Daniel alone is rewarded, without reference to his God; Belshazzar, unlike Nebuchadnezzar, is not interested in the source of Daniel's wisdom.

It is important to note, however, that the destruction of Belshazzar is not the last story in the cycle, so that it cannot be taken to mark the defeat of human kingship. The final note of this chapter brings the kindly Darius to the throne. The stories of Daniel, then, reflect degrees of hostility to Gentile monarchs, but nowhere is Gentile kingship rejected. These kings, good or evil, are appointed by God. Indeed, the arrangement of the stories places at the end the most positive depiction of a Gentile king. To individual kings God responds by persuading, meeting the challenge, or, in the last resort, destruction and replacement by another. But, overall, the stories affirm not only the *possibility*, but the *desirability* of Jews living in harmony under Gentile rulers. There is in principle no contradiction between the rule of the king and the rule of God. The king is, after all, God's appointed ruler.

The picture given by the stories is not, however, one of complete harmony. The vision in ch. 2 foresees an end to the sequence of kingdoms and the ultimate establishment of an eternal kingdom, that of God's own people. Yet this hope does not constitute a rejection of Gentile rule, for its fulfilment belongs only to the time appointed by God. In chs. 7–12, on the other hand, this appointed time is felt to have arrived, a belief occasioned by a breakdown in the harmony between Gentile king and God. A Gentile king has not only persecuted the Jews but, more significantly, committed sacrilege by abolishing the daily sacrifice. Hence, the end of the old dispensation is perceived, the 'time of deliverance' is at hand. It has been pointed out that while ch. 2 depicts the world empires as successively more decadent, from gold to iron and clay, ch. 7 represents the last as the most terrible of all. But it would be wrong to read into this the notion of increasingly antagonistic kingdoms culminating in the arch-enemy Antiochus. We are told only that the fourth kingdom was different from all the others (7.7), and these others are disposed of all together (v. 12). The notion of historical *progress* is not present here; rather, a kingdom has arrived which is of a different order: one which by spawning the arrogant 'horn' proclaims itself as the last, for it has abolished the old dispensation. In 10.20f. we find, indeed, the same fairly static view of the succession of empires symbolized rather more dramatically through 'princes'—commanders of the heavenly armies protecting their allotted nations. The succession is predetermined, and the struggle to which these verses refer is a warfare between the 'princes' of Israel, Gabriel and Michael, and the 'princes' of the sovereign nations, Persia and Greece. The survey of history in chs. 10–12 is in no way concerned with the condemnation of the kingdoms until the very last.

The logic of the visions is thus straightforward. The harmony between Gentile kingdoms, Jews and God, sustained in different ways in chs. 1–6, has been broken, since the present Gentile kingdom has set itself against Jews and against God. The climax of history is thus announced, and a new order is imminent. Three devices are used to justify this conclusion theologically: the four kingdoms scheme of ch. 2; the 'seventy years' of Jeremiah; and, finally (and rather crudely) a 'revelation' given to Daniel by an angel describing the detailed course of events towards the 'end'. In all of these a final, renegade king appears in the guise of a 'horn', 'one who makes desolate', and finally 'king of the north'.

The king as the final enemy of God

The epithet 'king of the north' evokes the famous poem of Ezekiel about Gog of Magog (chs. 38–39). God will bring Gog 'from the uttermost parts of the north', and lead him against the mountains of Israel, where he will fall (39.2). Gog is the personification of all Israel's foes (most of whom, in Israel's history, came from the north), and all Israel's military humiliations are concentrated into a single epic moment when God will destroy the foe among the mountains of Israel. Antiochus becomes, then, more than a Gentile monarch who challenges God: he is the arch-foe, the personification of all rebellion. Gog is described in Ezekiel 38 as summoning a force of many nations to come upon a quiet and peaceful Israel. Yet he is himself summoned by God, and through his defeat God will 'vindicate his holiness'. From these chapters of Ezekiel a new perspective is added to the portrayal of the Gentile king. From the earthly point of view, he schemes against an unsuspecting and vulnerable people, marching into their midst with a mighty host. From a more informed point of view, the king is not the protagonist, but the victim. It is God who moves him, and the purpose of it all is to manifest the glory of God.

In Daniel 8.8-12 we find another description of the last earthly king, also possibly alluding to an OT prophetic passage. Isaiah 14.12-20 compares the ascendancy of the Babylonian king to the mythical rise of the Day-Star (in Christian tradition, Lucifer, in Hebrew *Helal ben shahar*, 'son of dawn'), who led a rebellion in heaven, failed, and fell. In the words of Isaiah:

> You said in your heart . . . 'I will make myself like the Most High'.
> But you are brought down to Sheol, to the depths of the Pit. Those

who see you will stare at you, and ponder over you: 'Is this the man
who made the earth tremble, who shook kingdoms, who made the
world like a desert and overthrew its cities . . . All the kings of the
nations lie in glory, each in his own tomb; but you are cast out,
away from your sepulchre . . . '

Whether or not the writer of Daniel 8.8-12 has this passage in mind
(or, perhaps, the myth which lies behind it, though this is even less
certain), he is giving us a picture of a king who aspires not merely to
the destruction of the Jewish people, but to the overthrow of all other
kingdoms and ultimately to a divine status. Lebram has argued that
the complex figure of Antiochus in Daniel 7–12 exhibits many layers,
including the wise, cunning malefactor (8.23-25), the enemy of divine
order (ch. 7), enemy of the gods (11.37-39) and the eschatological foe
of Egypt (ch. 11). In unravelling the development of such a figure,
Lebram pays careful attention to Hellenistic (Egyptian and Syrian)
political and apocalyptic ideas. Whether or not his very detailed and
speculative treatment is convincing, there is abundant evidence that
the antagonism towards Antiochus reflected in Daniel makes sense
against a background of hostility towards Hellenistic monarchs,
especially in Egypt (see also Collins, pp. 192-93). In such a case as
this, however, we encounter the notorious difficulty of distinguishing
influences from parallels, and it is uncertain how much the Hellenistic
material contributes anything to the significance of the figure of
Antiochus in Daniel. It seems safer to lay emphasis on the figure of
the king in the book of Daniel as a whole, recognizing that the
eschatological royal villain of chs. 7–12 was most probably read
alongside Nebuchadnezzar and Belshazzar in the earlier part of the
book.

This last point brings us to another feature of the God-king conflict
in the stories, where God manifests both the power to deliver, and his
glory, in the face of challenge by Gentile kings. There is, of course, a
very large difference between the stories and visions in presenting the
outcome of this conflict. We must consider the implications of
juxtaposing the two treatments of Gentile monarchy in the same
book. Or, to approach the same point from another direction, we may
ask why the visions are attached to the stories (or vice versa). A
typological reading of the stories is available in the light of the
visions: Antiochus can be read into the figure of Nebuchadnezzar (or
the other kings). This typological dimension has been misinterpreted
by many scholars (Rowley being the outstanding example) as evidence

that the entire book is a unit written in Maccabean times. The wide differences between the two halves require other conclusions to be drawn. It does not seem plausible that the stories were *written* as veiled accounts of the Maccabean period. There is in the visions a totally new orientation towards Gentile monarchy according to which history has moved to a decisive stage from which it cannot move back. The ongoing challenge of human sovereignty is finally to be played out once and for all, with the Jew, as always, caught in the middle.

Further Reading

On the figure of Antiochus:

*Davies, *'Eschatology in the Book of Daniel'*.

J.C.H. Lebram, 'König Antiochus im Buch Daniel', *VT* 25 (1975), pp. 737-72.

8

THE JEWISH PEOPLE,
THE 'SON OF MAN'
AND THE 'HOLY ONES'

IN THE STORIES OF Daniel, the Jews are defined essentially by their religion, not by political allegiance or even nationality. Only in 2.44, which, of course, speaks of the future, do we find any allusion to a Jewish nation-state:

> And in the days of those kings the God of heaven will set up a
> kingdom which shall never be destroyed, nor shall its sovereignty
> be left to another people.

At the time of composition of the visions, the Jews were a nation in their own land, and accordingly they are corporately defined. Theologically, this definition is bound up with the terms 'son of man' and the 'holy ones of the Most High'. Therefore in this chapter we shall deal with the imagery and interpretation of the vision of ch. 7, one of the most controversial points of interpretation in contemporary biblical research.

The simplest way to analyse the problem is to take as the fundamental issue the question whether the final kingdom of the 'holy ones', which is received by 'one like a son of man' (or 'one in human form'?) is an earthly kingdom (the kingdom of the Jewish people) or a transcendent one (the kingdom of God or of angelic beings), in which earthly Israel is transformed. In ch. 2, although the text is not explicit, most scholars understand an earthly Jewish kingdom to be expected. In ch. 12, however, a transformation of *part* of Israel in a transcendental 'kingdom' seems to be anticipated. Where, between these two notions, does that of ch. 7 lie? The identity of the 'holy ones' and of the 'son of man' are the major elements in this fundamental problem.

In the interpretation of the vision, the 'son of man' is interpreted as the 'people of the holy ones of the Most High' (v. 27). In the middle of the chapter, vv. 19-22, where we have already noted a curious confusion of vision and interpretation (see ch. 5 above), we find, together with the 'ancient of days' and the 'horn', the 'holy ones of the Most High' instead of the 'son of man', reinforcing the impression that the two terms denote the same entity. But is it the case that the two terms are virtually interchangeable? Is the 'son of man' simply a symbol of the 'holy ones'? And who, after all, are the 'holy ones' (*or* 'people of the holy ones')?

The 'holy ones'

Let us take the identity of the 'holy ones' as our first question. The Aramaic *qaddîšîn* (= Hebrew *q^{e}dôšîm*: 'holy ones') is used in the OT and intertestamental Jewish literature primarily to denote angels, although it is also used of humans. Linguistically, then, the 'holy ones' of Daniel 7 may be Israel or angels. The latter view has gained ground in recent years. It was suggested in 1927 by Procksch, argued forcefully by M. Noth in 1955, and has been advocated more recently by Dequeker and Collins. The opposite view, which remains perhaps the most popular, has been vigorously defended by, among others, Brekelmans and Di Lella. It may be said that a conclusive verdict is difficult. The phrase 'people of the holy ones of the Most High' in v. 27, which is obviously a crucial element in the debate, is rather ambiguous evidence, for it can be argued either that this tends to distinguish the human 'people' from the heavenly 'holy ones', or, equally, that since both the 'holy ones' and the 'people of the holy ones' are given dominion, the terms are synonymous. The whole debate is further complicated by the possibility (see Chapter 5 above) that vv. 15-22 are, or contain, some secondary expansion of the original narrative. Accordingly, 'holy ones' and 'people of the holy ones' may be regarded as equivalent terms, but in different sources, for the same group. Again, in vv. 21-22, it is said that the horn 'made war with the holy ones and prevailed over them', apparently favouring the view that the 'holy ones' are human. Here Noth contended that the verses were secondary (mainly on the ground that 'holy ones' could not mean 'angels' here!); yet in v. 25, where, on his argument, the text *had* to refer to angels, he suggested, not very convincingly, that instead of 'prevailed', the verb might be better translated 'assailed'.

Although, as has been said, the arguments are not conclusive, a human reference is more likely on the evidence of ch. 7 taken alone. But the possibility of an angelic reference gains support from elsewhere, in particular 8.10-13:

> [The little horn] grew great, even to the host of heaven; and some of the host of the stars it cast down to the ground, and trampled upon them. It magnified itself, even up to the Prince of the host; and the continual burnt offering was taken away from him, and the place of his sanctuary was overthrown. And the host was given over to it . . . Then I heard a holy one speaking; and another holy one said to the one that spoke . . .

Clearly 'holy one' in this passage means 'angel'. ('People of the holy ones' in v. 24 may have a human reference, but the text is admittedly corrupt.) Now, according to Collins, the 'host of heaven' are the angels, the lord of whom is God himself, and consequently Antiochus is depicted as vanquishing the angels. However, Moore, and more recently Delcor, have proposed that the 'host' of ch. 8 is the pantheon of pagan gods whose sanctuaries Antiochus is reported to have destroyed (in 11.8 the 'king of the south' carries gods off to Egypt). This assault culminates in the attack on their 'prince', which they take to mean the Jewish God. There is a similar passage in 11.36 where the king shall 'magnify himself above every god, and shall speak astonishing things against the God of gods'; here too, either angels or pagan deities may be alluded to.

The arguments in this respect are also finely balanced. The situation has been reached where Antiochus appears to be fighting against the Jewish people, but possibly angels, in ch. 7 and against angels or pagan gods in ch. 8. We can achieve a consistent interpretation if, as Collins suggests, we take both the 'holy ones' in chs. 7 and 8, and the 'host' in ch. 8, as angels. As we have already seen, Collins has argued for a common 'mythic pattern' in chs. 7–12. But we have expressed doubts about the presence of this pattern (see Chapter 5), and it must be asked whether or not Collins is imposing a consistency which does not, or need not, exist. Is Antiochus' assault in ch. 7 and in chs. 8 and 10–12 described in identical terms? According to Collins, since Antiochus *is* described in Daniel as warring against angels, there is only one objection to taking 'holy ones' as angels in ch. 7, namely the phrase 'people of the holy ones' in 7.27. Now, since Collins has argued for the unity of ch. 7, he is more or less obliged to take the words as referring to the human Israel. As a way out of this dilemma he offers a choice of two hypotheses: either 'the heavenly host has already mingled with Israel'; or 'the kingdom is being realized at once on two levels' (p. 143). He accepts either (or both) and concludes that the 'people of the holy ones' are 'the faithful Jews who share in the eschatological triumph of the host', a sharing which 'can be variously expressed as assimilation to the host (Daniel 12) or as enjoying dominion over "everything under heaven" (Daniel 7)' (p. 146).

Collins thus adopts the view that the visions of Daniel employ a vertical symbolism, in which heavenly and earthly realities are correlated. It might be replied that symbolizing the Jewish people by a heavenly 'son of man' figure in ch. 7 is achieving precisely this. But for Collins the visions do not work by using heavenly symbols for earthly events and people: they portray both earthly and heavenly realities as *two dimensions of the same reality*. 'Angels are not symbols', he says, 'but real beings' (p. 140). The relationship between the earthly conflict involving the Jewish people on the one hand, and the heavenly conflict with the host on the other hand is, as we have seen, important in Collins's understanding of the book. He refers to the War Scroll from Qumran which describes angels and men joining together in battle, a battle which is both heavenly and earthly.

If Collins's view has been correctly understood, he is denying the use of symbolism here—the heavenly beings exist in their own right. Collins develops his theory further with an interpretation which is of central importance for his understanding of the visions of Daniel and, indeed, of apocalyptic. He proposes that the visions are concerned not with a temporal eschaton, that is, a fulfilment of the historical process, so much as with a vertical transformation of human existence, with 'dimensions of present experience'. To put this another way, the visions afford an escape from earthly reality not into the near future, but into the heavenly dimension of the present. The final dominion of the 'holy ones' is thus not (or not merely) the historical advent of an Israelite kingdom, but a heavenly order, angelic rule, a reality already capable of being apprehended.

Is ch. 7 to be understood in the way Collins suggests? Let us first remind ourselves that in the stories, we already find the monarch occasionally depicted as persecuting Jews and at the same time ranging himself against the Jewish God. Behind the 'earthly' reality of fiery furnaces and lions' dens is the 'heavenly' challenge to divine sovereignty. Collins's 'two-story universe' is already present here, although devoid of mythological colouring. Also present in these stories is Collins's 'realized eschatology', conveyed in at least two ways: first, the divine deliverance of the heroes is an affirmation not of future deliverance for the Jewish people, but of a certain quality of life available to every Jew, namely fidelity to the Jewish God; and second, the promotion to high office of the heroes at the end of the stories is an affirmation of the social and political value of that fidelity. The notion of a 'kingdom of holy ones' in more than one dimension is quite beautifully conveyed in ch. 2, where the immediate issue of sovereignty between king and God is sharpened by the prediction of a future, final, and everlasting kingdom. It is quite possible to find the same notion in the visions of Daniel *whether or not an angelic kingdom is actually depicted*. The specific exegetical question before us is whether ch. 7 portrays an angelic kingdom or, symbolically, a human one. For two reasons, Collins's interpretation is unlikely. First, the story is essentially about judgment on other kings, and one king in particular. It is difficult if not impossible to apply Collins' theory to the beasts and the horns, which cannot be other than symbols for earthly kings and kingdoms. Second, there is no hint in ch. 7 of a particular society within Israel who are to enjoy this kingdom, a group of 'faithful Jews' who may participate in the reality of heaven; nothing suggests that the 'people of the holy ones' are other than the entire nation of Israel. In both these respects, ch. 7 differs from ch. 12, where there is a distinct division within the nation, a judgment between individuals and a blessed group of 'wise'. In ch. 7 the argument is about nations; in ch. 12 about individuals. The differences are important, and because they are important, they betray an important shift in reaction to the historical crisis under Antiochus. Collins's argument depends upon the kind of consistency between ch. 7 and chs. 10–12 which cannot be assumed and, indeed, is difficult to demonstrate.

On the contrary, it is more probable that ch. 2 was known to the author of ch. 7 than that chs. 7–12 were written as a unit to express a consistent ideology; and given that ch. 7 is a conscious development of ch. 2, the 'holy ones' are more probably the nation of Israel than angels. The notion of an angelic kingdom is in any case rather novel, as Brekelmans has pointed out (p. 329; see also Kuhn, p. 92).

In ch. 7, then, it seems preferable for many reasons to understand the 'holy ones' who receive the kingdom as Israel; in chs. 8, 10 and 11 Antiochus is depicted as waging war against heavenly beings. Both descriptions are perfectly appropriate, and do not need to be harmonized.

The 'son of man'

If the 'holy ones' are Israel, is the 'son of man' a symbol for the nation of Israel, or an individual in his own right? 10.20-21 represents the sequence of earthly kingdoms as also a heavenly contest between 'princes' of these kingdoms. In 12.1 the final dominion of Israel is described as the rise of their 'prince', Michael. This, among other considerations, has led Collins to his view that the 'son of man' in ch. 7 is Michael, the prince of the angelic 'holy ones'. The possibility is enhanced in 8.15f., where the angel Gabriel is described as 'having the appearance of a man'. Although we have doubted whether the 'holy ones' are angels, the identification of the 'son of man' is not dependent on that equation, since at 12.1 Michael is described as 'the great prince who has charge of your people'—wording which might seem even more compatible with a human meaning for 'holy ones', if the 'son of man' and Michael are to be identified.

This identification is, of course, contested. 'Son of man' is certainly used in the Old Testament (e.g. Ps. 8) to mean 'human being', and it is frequently noticed that the central vision of ch. 7 contrasts a human figure with beasts who symbolize the previous kingdoms. (To take this argument further, note that according to Gen. 1.26ff. man is created to have dominion over all the beasts.) But if the beasts in ch. 7 represent *kings* and not kingdoms, should not the 'son of man' also be a royal figure, a 'messiah' perhaps? Possibly; but in the stories it is the rule of *God* which is contrasted with that of Gentile kings, and it would be consistent with that contrast for God to be regarded in ch. 7 as the king of the Jews. In any case, is it strictly true, despite v. 17, that the beasts symbolize kings? Their characteristics are those of successive *kingdoms*, and individual kings are represented, in the case of the fourth beast, by its horns. Quite conceivably the beasts symbolize either kings or kingdoms or both; if this degree of flexibility is allowed to the symbols, might not the 'son of man' also be both a corporate and an individual figure? The suggestion certainly breaks through many of the difficulties presented by the 'son of man' and disposes of much of the heated debate; but we must not reach immediately for such a conclusion without first asking whether the author may not have intended one meaning rather than another.

Collins and Lacocque have suggested that the figure of Michael in ch. 12 stands for the 'son of man' of ch. 7, an idea which had previously occurred to Schmidt in 1900. It has been suggested that the appearance of Michael in fact presupposes his introduction in ch. 7, but he has of course already been mentioned by name as the 'prince' of Israel in 10.20-21. That the author of ch. 12 nevertheless understood Michael to be the 'son of man' is quite probable; but from this it does not follow that the author of ch. 7 did (or, indeed, that the modern exegete should necessarily side with ch. 12 against ch. 7!). Collins's line of argument, as we have already observed, requires and assumes a unity of authorship among the visions which is improbable. Indeed, there is a clear discrepancy between the scheme of national 'princes' in 10.20-21, in which each kingdom succeeds to world dominion as its 'prince' is elevated, and the opposition in ch. 7 between the bestial representation of human monarchs or monarchies and the transcendent representation (by a human or divine figure) of a kingdom of 'holy ones'. Are all kingdoms 'angelic', succeeding one another as their 'princes' battle among themselves, or is the kingdom of the 'holy ones' qualitatively different from all its predecessors, as ch. 7 strongly implies? The argument that in ch. 7 the 'son of man' is Michael who leads the angelic 'holy ones' overlooks the different ways in which ch. 7 and chs. 10–12 look at the phenomenon of world kingdoms.

It is to be concluded, then, that the 'son of man' most probably functions as a symbol for the human 'holy ones', although there can be no certainty—and no consensus on this problem seems likely.

The 'son of man' as a figure drawn from myth

Separate from the *function* of the 'son of man' is the question of the *origin of the symbolism*, which has been located in various quarters, most commonly mythological. Schmidt saw in him the Babylonian god Marduk, elected king of the gods after his victory over the beasts of chaos, according to the Babylonian Creation Epic; Gunkel broadened this theory in proposing a more common body of mythology featuring a victorious god. From Persian mythology has been found Saoshyant, an eschatological restorer, and Gayomart, the first man, or 'Urmensch'. Even Mithras, the god from Asia Minor whose cult was so popular among Roman soldiers, has been invoked. Among the more popular derivations is the Canaanite god Baal. The 'son of man' 'comes with the clouds of heaven'; Baal is described as 'riding the clouds'. The 'ancient of days' is accordingly identified with Baal's father, the high Canaanite god El, who is called in the Ugaritic texts 'father of years' (*'b šnym*). Emerton has suggested a specific *Sitz im Leben* for the entire scene in Daniel 7, namely the Canaanite cult of El Elyon in Jerusalem, elements of which, it is often thought, were incorporated into the Yahwistic Temple liturgy. A major problem here is the availability of ancient Canaanite myth, in an integral form, to the authors of Daniel, rather than of mythic *motifs* whose original associations will be of variable relevance, if of any. These criticisms have been cogently expressed by Ferch.

One, or some, of the mythical derivations may in fact have been influential in the composition of the vision of Daniel 7. The investigation is of less value, of course, if the 'son of man' is a symbol, not an individual. Although many commentaries devote a good deal of space to the origins of the 'son of man' imagery, it is questionable how far the *origin* (which is always speculative) offers clues to the *meaning* of the various figures in Daniel 7, or, indeed, to the judgment scene as a whole. For more extensive comments on the presence of mythical elements in Daniel, see above, Chapter 5.

Further Reading

The angelic interpretation:

> Noth, 'The Holy Ones of the Most High'.

> L. Dequeker, 'The "Saints of the Most High" in Qumran and Daniel', *OTS* 18 (1973), pp. 133-62.

> *Collins, pp. 123-47; 167-84.

The corporate interpretation:

> C.H.W. Brekelmans, 'The Saints of the Most High and Their Kingdom', *OTS* 14 (1965), pp. 305-29.

> V.S. Poythress, 'The Holy Ones of the Most High in Daniel VII', *VT* 26 (1976), pp. 208-13.

> G.F. Hasel, 'The Identity of the "Saints of the Most High" in Daniel 7', *Biblica* 56 (1975), pp. 173-92.

*Hartman and Di Lella, pp. 85-102.

J. Coppens, *La relève apocalyptique du messianisme royal. II: Le fils d'homme vétéro- et intertestamentaire*, Leuven: University Press, 1983.

Ugaritic/Canaanite mythical background:

J.A. Emerton, 'The Origin of the Son of Man Imagery', *JTS* 9 (1958), pp. 225-42.

A.J. Ferch, 'Daniel 7 and Ugarit: A Reconsideration', *JBL* 99 (1980), pp. 75-86.

Other works referred to:

M. Delcor, *Le livre de Daniel*, Paris: Gabalda, 1971.

H.-W. Kuhn, *Enderwartung und gegenwärtiges Heil*, Göttingen: Vandenhoeck & Ruprecht, 1965.

G.F. Moore, 'Daniel viii 9-14', *JBL* 15 (1896), p. 194.

O. Procksch, 'Der Menschensohn als Gottessohn', *Christentum und Wissenschaft* 3 (1927), pp. 425-43.

N. Schmidt, 'The Son of Man in the Book of Daniel', *JBL* 19 (1900), pp. 22-28.

For a discussion of the 'son of man' in Daniel and other Jewish literature:

Russell, *Method and Message*, pp. 324-52.

9

THE 'WISE' AND
THEIR DELIVERANCE

AT THE CLOSE OF the book of Daniel comes a passage of four verses in which a group within Israel, called the 'wise', are promised an extraordinary deliverance (12.1-4). These four verses are arguably the most important in the book, for they contain the only unambiguous statement of belief in resurrection in the Old Testament. The four verses are problematic at almost every point and their radical conceptions are expressed with extreme brevity. In this chapter we shall ask who are the 'wise', and what is the nature of the 'deliverance' which is promised.

The 'wise'

Daniel 11.32-35 makes a basic distinction between those who 'know their God' and those who 'violate the covenant':

> He [the king] shall seduce with flattery those who violate the covenant; but the people who know their God shall stand firm and take action [i.e. perform those religious rites they have been forbidden to perform by the king]. And those among the people who are wise shall make many understand, though they shall fall by sword and flame, by captivity and plunder, for some days. When they fall, they shall receive a little help. And many shall join themselves to them with flattery; and some of those who are wise shall fall, to refine and to cleanse them and to make them white, until the time of the end, for it is yet for the time appointed.

This passage seems also to make a further distinction among those who do not 'violate the covenant'. The reference to a 'little help' and to those who 'join themselves to them with flattery' are taken by virtually every commentator as a disparaging reference to the Maccabean resistance. If this is so (see the following Chapter), the

reason is quite obvious: the time of deliverance is the time appointed
by God, and the death of the righteous in the meantime is to test and
purify them; hence active resistance would be neither theologically
appropriate nor politically effective. The advocacy of passive resistance is in harmony with the stories; the heroes are powerless to
defend themselves, but in any case their witness rests not on their
power to resist but the power of their God to assert his sovereignty.
This is the stance of the 'wise' in our passage; their rôle is not to lead
resistance, but to teach and to suffer: they 'make many understand'
and they (or some of them) 'fall'.

Chapter 12 adds a little about the 'wise':

> Those who are wise shall shine like the brightness of the firmament;
> and those who turn many to righteousness, like the stars for ever
> and ever.

This statement needs to be understood as having the parallel
structure characteristic of Hebrew poetry. In other words, the two
halves of the sentence complement one another: there are not two
groups and two rewards, but one. Hence, it is the wise whose
function it is to 'turn to righteousness' and they shall shine like the
brightness of the sky, or like stars.

In the phrase 'turn many to righteousness' we must surely
recognize an allusion to the 'Servant' in Isaiah 53.11: 'by his
knowledge shall . . . my servant make many to be accounted righteous';
here too is found the connection between wisdom (Hebrew *śkl, mśkl*)
and righteousness (Hebrew *ṣdq*). Nickelsburg has demonstrated the
extent to which the Servant furnished an archetype of the righteous
man in intertestamental traditions, especially those dealing with final
vindication. It is very likely, then, that the 'wise' in Daniel are cast in
the rôle of the Servant who understands, suffers, and 'makes righteous'.
But how do the wise 'make righteous' (or 'turn to righteousness' as
the RSV has)? In the case of the Servant, most scholars believe either
that his suffering is an atoning activity or that he bears it as a
representative of his people. Accordingly, he brings about the
'righteousness' or 'innocence' of others by accepting a just punishment. Is it, then, by their *sufferings* that the 'wise' in Daniel 'make
many righteous'? This is an improbable interpretation. Chapter 12
makes no explicit reference to the sufferings of the 'wise', and the
parallelism between 'those who are wise' and 'those who make many
righteous' suggests that it is wisdom and not suffering which 'makes

righteous'. Furthermore, in 11.33-35, where the suffering of the wise is mentioned, we are told both that the wise 'make many understand' and also that their 'fall' is 'to refine and to cleanse them'. It is therefore almost certain that the task of the 'wise' is to 'make righteous' by *making others understand*.

We come now to the second archetype of the 'wise', the hero of the court-tale. Nickelsburg has identified the motif of the 'wise courtier' as a formative influence on vindication traditions in intertestamental literature generally, and in the case of Daniel such influence is undeniable. Indeed, the association between the activity and the vindication of the 'wise' of chs. 11–12 and the wise heroes of chs. 1–6 is the key to the unity of the book. As we observed earlier, the wise heroes perform two functions: they give understanding (to the king), demonstrating the superiority of their wisdom over that of others and hence earning the vindication of high office; and they also suffer, or at least undergo trial, by virtue of which they are publicly vindicated. Perhaps we should stress the word 'trial'. In ch. 3 the heroes are put on trial for their faith in their God (vv. 15-18; cf. v. 28) in a furnace. Is it by this story that the words 'to refine and to cleanse them' are prompted? At all events, the stories show how it is the 'wise' who are called upon both to give understanding and to face suffering.

But in what sense, if any, do the heroes of the stories 'make righteous'? An answer is possible on two levels. Superficially it is the king who receives the benefit of their wisdom: he is given to understand his dream or to acknowledge the fragility of his own power. Also, the king could be said to be made righteous in that he 'blesses the God of Shadrach, Meshach and Abednego' and issues a decree in their favour (3.28f.), or 'praises and extols and honours the King of heaven' (4.37) having been told he must 'practise righteousness' (v. 27) or commands all subjects to 'tremble and fear before the God of Daniel' (6.26). On another level, it is the stories about the heroes which make the Jewish readers understand and be righteous, for of course it is they who need to learn that God is in control of history, has ordanied appropriate times and seasons, has assured his people of their ultimate vindication and is not forgetful of their suffering. Is this not indeed what we must suppose the 'wise' of Daniel 11 and 12 taught to the 'many'?

Deliverance

The remarkable transformation described in 12.1-4 is not the only statement of the book of Daniel on the subject of deliverance. Nor should it be interpreted outside the context of the book as a whole.

Notions of 'deliverance' in Daniel

While there are expressions in the Old Testament of the belief that there would one day be a deliverance for Gentiles and reconciliation between all nations worshipping the God of Israel, and even a belief that Israel was commissioned to bring this about, the horizons of Daniel do not extend so far. Deliverance is always of Jews. The view of Gentile kings in the stories of Daniel is indeed, as we have seen, a very positive one. God has given them their sovereignty, and they are therefore God's regents, and to be loyally served. But we have no instance of any attempt at conversion. In ch. 4 Nebuchadnezzar 'praises', 'extols' and 'honours' the 'King of heaven', but does not become his worshipper, much less become a Jew. In ch. 6 Darius commands his subjects to 'fear and tremble' before the 'God of Daniel', but not to join his congregation. Daniel is no proselytizer. These stories belong in a society of Jews who had no wish for the distinction between themselves and Gentiles to be removed. The idea that these various kings enjoyed sovereignty from God included the notion that they would also lose it to another appointee. There is ultimately no 'deliverance' for the Gentiles, but only for individual Jews and for the Jewish nation as a whole.

The notion of individual deliverance in the stories is in fact more apparent than real. Two stories tell of individual acts of deliverance, where the heroes are rescued from death. Yet the real purpose of these acts is clearly more than the rescue of a single Jew or a small group of Jews. They are a demonstration to the king, part of a trial of strength in which God asserts his supremacy. By means of this demonstration, the stories perhaps offer assurance to all Jews that their God is lord of history and of the world, but scarcely any serious hope of immunity from persecution. They offer the assurance that Jews may rise to the highest political office, but little prospect of such success for most. Even exalted office is no guarantee of security, of course; perhaps the reverse.

Deliverance is assured only in the ultimate sovereignty of the Jewish people. This prospect is at best implicit in the stories of Daniel, except for ch. 2, and even there its realization lies far ahead.

However, in ch. 7 this ultimate sovereignty assumes a new dimension in that the foreign kingdoms are presented as evil and judged, while the kingdom is given to 'holy ones'. The *ethical* contrast between the final kingdom and all those preceding it is an important new element.

In the last two chapters of Daniel further developments in the notion of 'deliverance' have taken place. There is no longer any question of a Jewish kingdom. Both 'Jewish' and 'kingdom' have required drastic redefinition, and the issue is now a deliverance of the true, wise 'Israel' from the oppression of the historical process.

The final deliverance: 12.1-4

The description in these verses is extremely sketchy, in striking contrast with the detail of the preceding events, and with the descriptions of 'that day' which may be found in the prophetic books of the Old Testament (e.g. Isa. 24–27; Ezek. 37; Joel 3; Zech. 13–14). Many of its phrases seem to be quotations of or allusions to other parts of the Old Testament, but their use seems to be intended to affirm that what is to come has been long foreseen rather than to clarify exactly what it is that will transpire. We have in fact a series of brief statements which hardly amount to a coherent description. Michael will 'stand', there will be a time of trouble, 'your people' will be delivered, 'many' who 'sleep in the dust of the earth' shall awake to everlasting life or everlasting contempt, and 'those who are wise' shall 'shine like the brightness of the firmament'. The various components require to be considered separately and carefully.

i. *Michael.* At what time will Michael 'arise' (or 'stand'), and what does his 'standing' entail? If, as seems apparent, he acts after the demise of the 'king of the north' in 11.45, then Michael is not the vanquisher of the king, but commences his rôle only after that king's death. The 'rise' of Michael does not therefore include the conquest of the king. Two interpretations of Michael's function are possible, however: forensic and military. Nickelsburg, while discerning both elements, has laid strress on the forensic character of Michael's eschatological role, as presiding over the final judgment in which the righteous are vindicated and the wicked punished. The idea of an angel who defends the interests of the righteous in heaven is widely represented in intertestamental literature. A very similar function, for example, is assigned to the heavenly Melchizedek in the Qumran Melchizedek fragment (11QMelch), and many scholars believe that

Michael and Melchizedek are the same figure in different guises (the figure may well be reflected the Johannine Paraclete: *paraklētos* is a forensic term). According to Nickelsburg such a figure can be traced back to Zechariah 1.12, where an 'angel of the Lord' pleads with Yahweh to end his seventy years' anger at Israel. The forensic meaning of the Hebrew verb (*'āmad*) is probably also found in Psalm 82.1, where God passes sentence on the gods (= the 'princes' in Daniel's vocabulary) of the nations. On Nickelsburg's view, Michael's rôle is to ensure Israel's final vindication and the condemnation of its enemies.

Another view of Michael's rôle, however, can be derived from 10.13, 20f., where this angel is fighting against the angelic 'princes' of Persia and then of Greece. His 'standing' in 12.1 may then mean that his supremacy over the other 'princes' has been achieved, and that the sovereignty of his people, Israel, has now dawned. It is possible, by reading 11.45 and 12.1 together, to gain the impression that Antiochus comes to his end by the agency of Michael, or even to understand by the 'time of trouble' which follows Michael's 'rise' a battle between Israel's angel and the Syrian persecutor. Yet in ch. 10 it is another angel (vv. 5-6) who undertakes the fighting, and Michael is only a helper. The evidence thus suggests that Michael is *not* Israel's warrior, and that his own rôle, in Daniel, is not essentially a military one. This conclusion is even more probable if the author of chs. 10–12 saw in Michael the 'son of man' of ch. 7, for he also receives his dominion after the destruction of the beasts, and is not himself their destroyer.

In Zechariah 3.1ff. the advocate angel is opposed by the accusing angel, Satan (who has the same rôle in Job), and in numerous intertestamental texts we find a pair of opposing angels, whether they function judicially, militarily or in both ways. Accordingly, it has been suggested that in Daniel too we should look for a counterpart to Michael. Nickelsburg suspects that behind Antiochus lies such a figure, the 'chief demon', but this is one of several respects in which Nickelsburg's stimulating but sometimes confusing enquiry carries speculation far beyond the evidence of the texts.

We have to conclude, therefore, that references to Michael at 12.1 and in ch. 10 leave his precise rôle open to debate, although we can be confident of the point that is being made in 12.1: the end of the present terrible oppression will come about by agencies in heaven and not on earth; there will be a final demonstration not only of God's sovereignty, but also of his justice.

ii. *'A time of trouble'*. The words are taken from Jeremiah 30.7:

> Alas! that day is so great there is none like it; it is a time of distress
> for Jacob; yet he shall be saved out of it.

But what is the 'trouble' here? It is possible that what is being described is the throes of the conflict between Antiochus and Michael; one may not be too pedantic about the sequence of events between 11.45 and 12.1, especially since the clumsy repetition of 'at that time ... till that time; but at that time' in 12.1 makes a precise sequence difficult to discern. Nevertheless, we may understand that this 'trouble' exceeds what has ever been 'since there was a nation' because the fall of Antiochus means more than the shift of world sovereignty from one kingdom to another: it is the end of the entire process, the point at which God definitively imposes his own sovereignty directly upon human affairs. It is the 'day of the Lord' to which the Old Testament prophets are seen to have referred. The end of Antiochus is merely the *prelude* to this 'trouble'. Possibly the author knew well that the death of the persecutor (had it in fact occurred before these words were written?) would not by itself resolve the problem, which had now *become an internal crisis among the Jews*, and giving rise to such distinct entities as the 'violators of the covenant' and the 'wise'. The intervention of Michael vindicates not the Jews, but the righteous. A 'time of trouble' even after the fall of Antiochus highlights an important shift in the problem with which the whole book of Daniel is concerned. In the stories, the question is 'how is the kingdom exercised in the life of the Jew?'; in the visions, 'when will the eschatological realization of the kingdom take place?'; and now, in ch. 12, with the destruction of Antiochus already disposed of, 'what will the eschatological kingdom mean?' Put less precisely, but more simply, we move from 'how?' to 'when?' to 'what?'

iii. *'Your people shall be delivered'*. Two questions are provoked by this phrase: who are 'your people', and what is entailed by 'deliverance'? It is evident that neither question is now answerable in nationalistic terms: 'your people' is not the nation Israel, and deliverance is not the nation's earthly sovereignty. Instead, those who are to be delivered have been already named 'in the book'. The notion of such a book is as old as Exodus 32.32, though a more direct influence may be Isaiah 4.3. Its presence here reinforces the predestinarian tone of Daniel, set by the stories no less than by the visions: as God has ordained the whole course of history, so he must also have foreknowledge of those who are to enjoy final deliverance. It is those presently alive, however, who are the concern. Yet the nature of their 'deliverance' is not spelled out. Does it consist, for instance, of 'eternal life'? The text leaves it to the reader—ancient or modern—to hope, or interpret, as he will.

iv. *'Many of those who sleep . . . '* The phraseology here is perhaps influenced by Isaiah 26.19, a poetical text which can hardly be taken as a literal description of resurrection. But, as Ginsberg pointed out, even in Isaiah this revival is set between an appeal for deliverance (vv. 16ff.) and an announcement of God in judgment (vv. 20ff.)— which may be a guide to the interpretation of our passage. Nickelsburg stresses, quite correctly, that the resurrection here is not vindication in itself, for both righteous and wicked will 'awake'. The vindication, which is the *purpose* of the resurrection, comes both in the restoration of life to the righteous and the shame of those who once persecuted them: there is, as it were, by the act of judgment a reversal of the past in which those who inflicted suffering bear shame and those who suffered enjoy life. 'Life' and 'death' throughout the Old Testament are used to convey more than existence and non-existence respectively. Death is present in sorrow, fear, alienation, sickness, while life is prosperity, health, longevity, happiness and security. The notion of eternal life is not to be reduced to that of immortality, which for the authors of Daniel is no benefit in itself. It is the quality, the content of one's existence which matters, and the righteous here are promised eternal blessing while the wicked will bear an eternal curse. Only the former condition deserves to be called 'life'.

The description of the fate of the wicked probably draws upon yet another prophetical text, Isaiah 66.24:

> And they shall go forth and look on the dead bodies of the men that have rebelled against me; for their worm shall not die, their fire shall not be quenched, and they shall be an abhorrence to all flesh [The word 'abhorrence' is reproduced in Daniel 12.2 as 'contempt'].

Scholars divide over the Hebrew word *rabbîm*, which usually means 'many', but is probably used at times to mean 'all'. Which is meant here is difficult to decide: 'those who sleep' falls between 'every one whose name shall be found written in the book' and 'those who are wise', both of which are restricted categories. A universal resurrection is probably not envisaged, not even a universal Jewish resurrection. 'Many' is a preferable translation, but raises a further problem—are they a defined group? *Rabbîm* in 11.33 and 12.3 denotes the recipients of the teaching of the 'wise', and one might therefore be tempted to the think of these *rabbîm* as disciples of the wise. But in 11.34 we have 'many shall join themselves to them with flattery', and in v. 35 'some of those who are wise'. It seems as if such vague references are part of the idiom of ch. 10–12 in which individuals, groups and nations are not identified by name. One might aptly call it an 'oracular' idiom. It is up to the reader to define the 'many' and the 'some' if he wishes.

But in the last analysis, it is the reader himself who is challenged to identify himself with the 'wise'. Daniel is instructed to complete his book and seal it until the time of the end (12.4, 9). In the interim much will happen; both wickedness and knowledge will increase. ' . . . none of the wicked shall understand; but those who are wise shall understand' (v. 10). In thus addressing Daniel, of course, the angel addresses the reader. Reading Daniel, *does he understand?* If so, he is among the 'many'.

v. *'Those who are wise . . . '* The identity of the 'wise' we cannot learn directly from this text, but only from the book as a whole. We shall consider this question in the next chapter. Here we shall direct our attention towards their fate. We have already noted that 'shining like the brightness of the firmament' and 'like the stars' are not to be taken as two distinct destinies unless the 'wise' and 'those who turn many to righteousness' are different groups, which is improbable. But certainly this group is promised a pre-eminence among the restored Jewish people which it enjoys while still awaiting the end. Most probably we are to understand 'brightness' and 'like stars' as figurative descriptions of this pre-eminence. However, Collins interprets the phrases literally, arguing that the group in question will be transformed and given an angelic status, noting, correctly, that angels are often depicted as stars. The suggestion harmonizes with his thesis that the 'saints' in ch. 7 are an angelic host in which righteous Jews also participate, and with his more general theory that 'apocalyptic thinking' is characterized by a particular understanding of earthly and heavenly interaction.

Much, of course, depends on the plausibility of Collins's understanding of Daniel 7 and of 'apocalyptic thinking'. In this particular case, he has chosen to discount the parallelism of the two-part description, focussing on 'stars' only—and also disregarding the presence of the word 'like'. He wishes to translate '*as* the stars' (effectively 'as stars [= angels]'. But this entails translating also 'as the brightness of the firmament', as if the 'brightness' is what the 'wise' will become rather than what they will shine *like*. We must conclude that, again, we are not being told very much at all about the nature of the lot of the 'righteous': they are being offered a hope of glory but not a prescribed status.

vi. '*But you, Daniel . . .*' It is most appropriate that the destiny of the 'wise' should be rounded off with a reference to the destiny of the archetypal wise man. But like Daniel himself, we are reminded of the 'words' and the 'book'. The fiction of hiding away a book until the time for which it is written is, of course, a standard pseudepigraphic device. But there is more to it than that. For the book itself contains the true teaching of the 'wise': Daniel is not *about* understanding and 'making righteous'; it performs that function itself. The second half of this verse, whatever its words mean precisely, appears to be drawing a contrast between the search for knowledge which will continue in the interim, and the true wisdom which is locked away in Daniel's book: ' . . . none of the wicked shall understand; but those who are wise shall understand'. These words of the angel address, through Daniel, the reader of his book; does he understand, or not? Is he, then, wicked, or wise? The contrast of 'wicked' and 'wise' here is not unexpected or out of place. Daniel's wisdom and righteousness are one, and the basic ethic which equates wisdom and virtue is that of Old Testament wisdom as found in Proverbs, where the wicked man is also the fool.

With v. 4, it is widely suspected, the book of Daniel once ended. What follows is rather an anticlimax: the calculation of the end is revised and the lessons about understanding and suffering are reiterated, the book now ending with a recapitulated instruction to Daniel to go his way and await his allotted place. No new light is shed on the problems of 12.1-4, and it is best to be content with what is said. In the end, the vagueness of the hope is undoubtedly deliberate; but the vagueness in no way diminishes the wisdom which nourished the hope.

Daniel and the problem of theodicy

The problem with which the whole of Daniel, but especially chapter 12, deals is theodicy, the righteousness of God. We have seen how the stories in Daniel affirm the righteous sovereignty of God, yet in a context where the individual Jew could not expect complete freedom from persecution, nor, it seems, any ultimate personal reward. This ethic is perhaps one of the most noble in the entire Bible, but it was found wanting by those suffering under Antiochus. It has been shown already that the problems, the answers, the literary forms and devices of the visions of Daniel are very largely determined by the stories to which they were obviously composed in order to be attached.

But Daniel's answer to the problem of theodicy cannot be appreciated without a wider perspective. While much of the Old Testament assumes that a man receives his rightful deserts, the book of Job challenged such a view, as did the author of Ecclesiastes. At a time of persecution, the problem became acute: what good did a martyr's death achieve? One answer is offered in the second book of Maccabees, written in Greek about a century after Daniel. Here the righteous martyr both achieves salvation for his people by averting the divine wrath which has occasioned the persecution, and is assured that the body which he offers up will be restored to him by God. On the other hand, the first book of Maccabees, written in Hebrew several decades after Daniel, praises a noble death, but finds its only benefit in its contribution to national restoration, for it holds no hope of reward beyond the grave. By comparison, Daniel's response is not at all developed, and perhaps not entirely coherent, possibly betraying the beginnings of a doctrine which came to full expression only later.

It seems clear, in the end, that Daniel's notion of deliverance nevertheless depends less on a specific belief in a certain kind of vindication than in a mode of belief, 'understanding'. It may be too much to say that for Daniel to understand how God's sovereignty and justice operate is sufficient, but this is surely close to the truth. What is to be 'understood', of course, goes beyond the categories of the rest of the Old Testament: it is not divine words from prophets, it is not the sacred history of God's chosen people; it is not even the worldly wisdom of the sages who wrote proverbs. It is the secrets, the mysteries of God's dealings with the world, revealed to the sage by God or his deputies. It is transmitted by the wise, in literary form, to those who may hear and be delivered at the End. Perhaps in Daniel we may already see the roots of that religious propensity called 'gnosticism', which proclaimed that things were not as they seemed, and that deliverance from a wicked world was attainable only through esoteric 'knowledge' (*gnōsis*). Yet in Daniel, such knowledge was not to be divorced from devout obedience to God's laws, nor did it deny the reality of the world of kings and politicians. But in the end, Daniel is not, like the contemporary 'apocalypses' of the Hellenistic world, a political document, for in its final chapter it passes beyond all political or national categories, and speculates—this is surely the correct word—on the transcendence of the whole order of history and nature, affirming, however allusively, that divine justice and sovereignty will be asserted, even beyond the limits of human experience and imagination.

Further Reading

*Collins, pp. 191-218.

G.W.E. Nickelsburg, *Resurrection, Immortality and Eternal Life in Intertestamental Judaism*, Cambridge: Harvard University / London: OUP, 1972.

H.L. Ginsberg, 'The Oldest Interpretation of the Suffering Servant', *VT* 3 (1953), pp. 400-404.

10

THE AUTHORS

IN THE 'WISE' OF Daniel 11–12 we see the authors of Daniel, those who during the troubled years preceding the Maccabean rebellion added to a group of stories about an exilic hero a series of visions attributed to him, the purpose of which was to apply the ideology of the stories to the particular circumstances of their own time. What we are told of the 'wise', then, we can apply to the authors: they were not of those who 'violated the covenant' (11.32), but neither did they believe in active resistance. They preferred to wait until the time appointed by God should arrive and to accept what persecution came their way as a test of their loyalty. They were teachers, giving understanding, and their purpose was to 'make righteous'.

There is more that we can deduce about these 'wise'. They were fervent supporters of the cult. It is the cessation of the twice-daily burnt offering which is the focus of concern in chs. 7–12, and not the other ingredients of Antiochus' proscription of Judaism, such as the ban on circumcision, burning of books of the Law, or forced eating of pork. In ch. 9 the holy city and the Temple (vv. 24, 26), and the removal (slaughter?) of a High Priest (an 'anointed one, a *māšîah*, v. 26) are the evident focus of the recitation of events. The authors, then, if not priests, held the holy city, its Temple and its cult, in great esteem.

Did these authors belong to an identifiable group? Most scholars think so, and a large number of these would give to this group the name *Hasidim* or 'Hasideans' ('pious'). However, this name has been applied so indiscriminately that its use tells us virtually nothing. Let us therefore concentrate on three classes of which contemporary or near-contemporary sources speak.

1. *'Hasideans' (1 Maccabees 2.42; 7.12f.)*

We are told in these passages of some Hasideans, a group of whom joined the Maccabean family in their resistance, and are noted as 'mighty warriors of Israel, every one who offered himself willingly for the law'. Later when a group of scribes approached the High Priest and the Syrian general to seek terms, we are told that 'the Hasideans were the first among the sons of Israel to seek peace from them'. Both references are difficult to translate, but from them most scholars have drawn a picture of a party or sect of especial piety which having at one time espoused the cause of active resistance later became disillusioned and withdrew. When commentaries speak of the authors of Daniel as Hasideans (or Hasidim) it is to this group that they refer. Why the improbable identification persists is hard to explain. The writers of Daniel hardly qualify as 'mighty warriors', and there is nothing in Daniel which suggests that its authors were ever attracted to active resistance. Why the Hasideans sought peace is not stated, and it is only a conjecture that they played no further part in the active resistance. 2 Maccabees in fact suggests the opposite, and depicts them as forming the bulk of Judas Maccabee's army (14.6). We are nowhere told that they were teachers, or that they suffered especial persecution, while the description 'devoted to the law' is no more nor less appropriate to the writers of Daniel than to the Maccabees themselves.

2. Those *'seeking righteousness and justice'* (*1 Maccabees 2.29-38*)

The first reference to the Hasideans is preceded by an episode in which a group 'seeking righteousness and justice' went into the wilderness and stayed there with their families and possessions. Pursued by the royal forces, they remained in their hiding places, where they were attacked on the Sabbath, offering no resistance. It is often suggested that these are the Hasideans, but there is nothing at all to suggest such an identification. The story ends with the decision of Mattathias, the leader of the resistance, that he and his followers would in future fight on the Sabbath if necessary. Now, the passive behaviour of this group is rather more consistent with the attitude of Daniel than the Hasideans. But we have very little else by way of positive correlation. We are told that they had found their circumstances unbearable, but this is just as likely to have been due to their strict obedience to the law as to any concentrated persecution. The action of withdrawing to avoid trouble is not consistent with Daniel's presentation of the 'wise' as teachers. One would have expected such teachers to stay with their disciples among the people and endure persecution, like their hero Daniel, rather than to run away. 'Seeking righteousness and justice' is certainly applicable to the ethos of Daniel, but it is so unspecific that it could apply to any number of Jews, including Maccabees and Hasideans.

3. *The scribes (Ben Sira)*

It is in the apocryphal book of Jesus ben Sira (or Ecclesiasticus) that we find the words of a professional scribe of the beginning of the second century BC. Heaton in particular has argued in the introduction to his commentary on Daniel that Ben Sira is the ancestor of the 'wise' of Daniel (he equates the scribes with the Hasideans, but that identification is irrelevant to the issue at hand). According to Ben Sira, the business of the scribe is as follows (39.1-3; 6-8):

> ... He who devotes himself to the study of the law of the Most
>   High
> will seek out the wisdom of all the ancients,
> and will be concerned with prophecies;
> he will preserve the discourse of notable men
> and penetrate the subtleties of parables;
> he will seek out the hidden meanings of proverbs
> and be at home with the obscurities of parables
>
> ...
> If the great Lord is willing,
> he will be filled with the spirit of understanding;
> he will pour forth words of wisdom
> and give thanks to the Lord in prayer.
> He will direct his counsel and knowledge aright,
> and meditate on his secrets.
> He will reveal instruction in his teaching,
> and will glory in the law of the Lord's covenant.

There are certainly similarities here to the kinds of activity undertaken in the book of Daniel—the study of the 'wisdom of the ancients', concern with 'prophecies', 'instruction in teaching' and possession of a 'spirit of understanding' may all be appropriately attributed to the 'wise' who were responsible for Daniel. Included in this account of the scribe, moreover, is the statement that 'he will serve among great men and appear before rulers' (v. 4), which would apply to Daniel. Ben Sira also shares a reverence for the cult and the high priest (see chapter 50).

On the other hand, as has been frequently pointed out, Ben Sira did not believe in a life after death, did not actually recount any visions, and seemed concerned more with the practical wisdom of everyday life than with the meaning of history; he even seemed to discourage speculation about such things (3.21-24):

> Seek not what is too difficult for you,
> nor investigate what is beyond your power.
> Reflect upon what has been assigned to you,
> for you do not need what is hidden.
> Do not meddle in what is beyond your tasks,
> for matters too great for human understanding have been shown you.
> For their hasty judgment has led many astray,
> and wrong opinion has caused their thoughts to slip.

Finally, Ben Sira's term for the scribe is *sōpēr*, not *maśkîl*, as it is in Daniel.

Many of the differences between Ben Sira and Daniel can be accounted for by the drastic nature of the events which intervened between the two writings. Radical revisions of teaching and major developments in the function of the scribes are not to be ruled out. But with all due allowance, the most that can be allowed in this direction is that the writers of Daniel came from the same broad circle as Ben Sira. Before we can give a more positive assessment, we must await further research on the character of Jewish wisdom traditions in Judaism of the Persian and Hellenistic period, and in particular the place of speculative wisdom such as that of Enoch, for example, in it.

A fourth possibility remains, namely that the authors of Daniel belonged to a group, distinct but hitherto unrecognized. There are affinities between writings such as parts of Enoch and some of the Dead Sea Scrolls which may point to a stream within Judaism within which speculations about the mysteries of the universe and of history were cultivated. Many elements in this speculation can be traced back to the Eastern Diaspora—certain calendrical traditions, knowledge of astronomy, dualism, for example. In particular, the use of *maśkîl* as the title of an office at Qumran (or so it seems) has frequently been noted; less frequently noted is the use of *rabbîm* to designate the community. It is at present too early to attempt to define such a group, if it existed, but the presence of some of these elements in Daniel, together with the Babylonian setting and Diaspora provenance of the stories, offers an area of investigation in which studies of Daniel might fruitfully be pursued during the next decades.

The author and the reader

No discussion of the authors of Daniel ought to leave out of consideration the reader. The relationship between author and reader is a crucial concern in current biblical exegesis, and rightly so. The identity of the original readers of Daniel is no more certain than that of the author, but in a book which functions so evidently as a didactic work the relationship between the author/teacher and reader/disciple is worth a look. In this regard, one element of the book's technique deserves special attention. In the first six chapters the author stands behind his main character, Daniel, and presents the reader with an external, historical world far removed in time from his own. Here the relationship between author and reader is at its most distant. The reader sees Daniel as a hero of a narrative, in a relatively objective manner of relationship. In chapters 7–12 this hero is no longer the object of the reader's attention but its subject: he is the 'author' and speaks about himself. The reader now confronts the hero directly, and the third party author of the tales has vanished. The world which now embraces Daniel and reader changes too, for it is now an internal world—and insofar as it includes the external world, that world progressively approaches the reader's own. The reader is thus drawn into a closer and less objective manner of relationship to Daniel: he can identify with Daniel more closely and finds himself directly spoken to. He is not an observer of the exploits of Daniel, but the privileged confidant. At the very end of chapter 12, the author Daniel slips away. He is to 'go his way'; others will 'understand' if they are wise. The reader is now effectively addressed by the angel himself, and the process of absorbing the reader into the book has been completed. Whether or not this process is deliberate (and why not?) it can be quite objectively perceived. It is, of course, a well-known didactic art to move from objective description towards personal confrontation, and by its use, the book of Daniel achieves its goal of imparting that wisdom which will 'turn many to righteousness'.

Further Reading

On the Hasidim:

O. Plöger, *Theocracy and Eschatology*, Oxford: Blackwell, 1968.

M. Hengel, *Judaism and Hellenism*, London: SCM Press, 1974, I, pp. 175-218.

P.R. Davies, 'Hasidim in the Maccabean Period', *JJS* 28 (1977), pp. 127-40.

For links between Ben Sira and Daniel:

*Heaton, *Daniel*, pp. 19-24.

On relevant trends in postexilic Judaism:

*M. Stone, *Scriptures, Sects and Visions*, Oxford, Blackwells, 1982, pp. 37-47, 57-70.

INDEXES

INDEX OF ANCIENT SOURCES

Old Testament

Non-Biblical

INDEX OF SUBJECTS

INDEX OF AUTHORS